Dog Dilemmas

Pet Peeves

Dog Dilemmas

Simple Solutions to Everyday Problems

GARY R. SAMPSON, DVM, with DICK WOLFSIE

emmis

books

For further information, contact the publisher at

 Emmis Books
1700 Madison Road
Cincinnati, OH 45206
www.emmisbooks.com

Library of Congress Cataloging-in-Publication Data

Sampson, Gary R.
  Dog dilemmas / Gary R. Sampson with Dick Wolfsie.
    p. cm. -- (Pet peeves)
  ISBN 1-57860-226-2
  1. Dogs--Behavior. 2. Dogs--Training. I. Wolfsie, Dick. II.
Title. III. Series.
  SF433.S265 2005
  636.7'0887--dc22
                                      2004030424

Designed by Andrea Kupper
Edited by Jessica Yerega

DEDICATION

I dedicate this book to all the veterinarians who have shared their practices with me by referring clients and patients, thus keeping me challenged and deepening my knowledge of the behavior of dogs.

And to my beloved pet Elaine, my wife of forty-seven years, who encouraged me to share my stories.

And, finally, to all my dogs over the years— Bonnie, Duffy, Heidi, Schultz, Liesel, and Lizzie—thank you. You all taught me so much.

Contents

Introduction.. viii

Barney, Dick Wolfsie, and Me....................................xi

Part One: Aggression

Chapter 1: Noah's Bark................................... 18

Chapter 2: Oscar the Grouch......................... 23

Chapter 3: Q.E. Louie.................................... 28

Chapter 4: Hounded by a Beagle.................... 33

Chapter 5: The Hand That Feeds You............38

Chapter 6: Dutch Treats................................ 44

Chapter 7: Golden Years................................ 49

Chapter 8: Doing It to the Max..................... 54

Chapter 9: Puppygate....................................59

Part Two: Anxiety

Chapter 10: Jay Walking................................66

Chapter 11: Thunder Dog.............................. 70

Chapter 12: Tale of a Tail............................. 74

Chapter 13: Home Alone................................78

Chapter 14: Little Mac................................... 83

Chapter 15: Fraidy Dog................................. 88

Chapter 16: Primrose Path.............................. 93

Chapter 17: A New Leash on Life...................97

Part Three: Housebreaking/Elimination Problems

Chapter 18: Dear John..................................... 106

Chapter 19: Whiz Kid...................................110

Chapter 20: Double Dribble........................... 115

Chapter 21: Fine for Littering....................... 119

Part Four: Destructive Behavior

Chapter 22: Being a Little Chewsy.................126

Chapter 23: Gold Diggers...............................130

Part Five: Other Misbehaviors

Chapter 24: No Barking Allowed....................136

Chapter 25: Star Search................................. 140

Chapter 26: Herd of Cats............................... 144

Chapter 27: The Two Faces of Mike............... 148

Chapter 28: Lickity Split................................152

Chapter 29: Sam the Sham............................155

Introduction

As a veterinarian who limits his practice to dog and cat behavior modification, I have been dealing with the misbehavior of humans for twenty years.

Of course, humans are not completely responsible for the conduct of their pets. All animal behavior is a curious combination of the animal's instincts and the effects of the conditions he is raised in. But, yes, *you* are the conditions.

The relationship between man and dog goes back tens of thousands of years. And both parties are pretty happy with the arrangement. Humans acquired an animal capable of great loyalty, one that would act not just as a companion, but as a protector and hunter. Dogs got a pretty good deal, as well. It's a lot easier to wait for your food to be put in a bowl than it is to stalk a wildebeest. And I kind of think that getting scratched behind the ears was the dog's idea.

Over time, the dog became more and more domesticated, gradually moving from the barn, to the porch, to the kitchen, and finally into the bedroom. The canine's distinctive personality became part of the family dynamics. Now, when I hear about dogs that sleep under the covers with their owners, I wonder if things haven't gone too far.

In fact, this is probably the reason you have bought this book. You have a dog that does not fit your image of how a family pet should behave. Your sheltie barks too much; your doxie isn't housebroken; your boxer chews the antique chair leg. These are pretty common problems, but, as you will discover, every dog is different. Every owner is different. Every situation is different.

My role is to help people understand why a 110-pound rottweiler is afraid of a thunderstorm and a 10-pound poodle chases the 200-pound mailman. If there were simple solutions to these problems, I would just fax my clients a checklist of do's and don'ts. But it doesn't work that way.

In our first phone conversation, I want the owner to tell me all about the dog. Among other things, I inquire about the dog's background and how he fits into the family. Of course, I also want to know exactly what the problem is and how it has been dealt with up to this point.

I am not content with just offering a solution. I want my clients to understand why the problem exists, because it gives them a better appreciation of how my directions for addressing the issue have a pretty good chance of working.

My suggestions are successful *only* when the client is willing and able to make a commitment to change his or her behavior—because only then will the dog's behavior change. That's not always easy. For example, I may tell a client *not* to pick up his Chihuahua when he is trembling out of fear. "That's the worst thing you can do," I'll say. That's tough for some people, but that's where a full explanation is so important. Then when the client says, "Oh, *now* I see why you said that," that's a pretty good indication my advice has been heard and understood. By the way, don't pick up your Saint Bernard either, but this time I have two good reasons.

Every day in this country, thousands of people abandon their dogs or relinquish them to humane

societies and animal shelters. Why? Because their dog
has a behavior problem that they cannot deal with. And
sadly, it is probably a behavior problem they contributed
to or are inadvertently reinforcing. That's where I come
in. The people who call me love their pets and are looking
for assistance. But for the thousands of people each year
who might give up on their dogs, I hope this book will be
a wake-up call that help is available.

All the stories are based on real cases, though on
occasion I have combined incidents so that a more typical
example can be represented. You'll meet a dog who loved
to catch moles and one that was scared of birds—just a
parade of quirky behaviors that stumped my clients but
will both amuse you and educate you about your pet.

By the way, if your dog loves to chew paperbacks, make
sure he can't reach this one. And don't miss Chapter
22. Now *there's* a dog that could sink his teeth into a
good book.

Barney, Dick Wolfsie, and Me

Although I have worked with thousands of dog and cat owners, I am probably best known for the six minutes I spent on a TV show with Dick Wolfsie in the fall of 1992. That episode is chronicled in Dick's book about his infamous dog. People ask me about it even now, years later.

Dick found Barney on his front step in 1991, and it wasn't long before the renegade little pooch was eating, chewing, and digging himself into deep trouble. Because Dick's wife could not tolerate the dog's destructiveness, she "encouraged" Dick to take Barney with him to work each morning during his show on WISH-TV.

At that time, I was beginning a new chapter in my life, as well. For thirty years I had been employed as an industrial veterinarian working to develop animal health products. But beginning in the mid-'80s, I decided to develop a veterinary practice limited to dog and cat behavior problems—always an interest of mine.

I had been watching Dick Wolfsie on TV for several years and, like so many viewers, was captivated by his new TV companion. For me, their relationship was especially endearing because as a young boy, I, too, had a beagle. His name was Duffy.

I believe all beagle owners deal with similar problems. Beagles are a spirited, inquisitive, high-energy breed that will love you to death, but also be the death of you. They are diggers, chewers, chow hounds, and escape artists. That's how I remembered Duffy. Duffy was also the neighborhood stud. In fact, I used Duffy the "love machine" as a way to make money to purchase my first car, renting out Duffy's services to people who wanted to breed beagles.

Duffy also did occasional freelance work, sometimes gone days at a time. My mother kept a calendar of which dogs in the neighborhood were in heat, so if Duffy missed a meal (which beagles seldom do) she'd have a pretty good idea of what had detained him and where I should go to get him.

Gary Sampson and Duffy, circa 1950.

At the suggestion of his veterinarian, Dick called me in search of some answers on how to stop Barney's incessant digging and chewing.

Despite my normally reticent demeanor, Dick somehow convinced me to come on live television and discuss the problems he was having with Barney. To this day, I don't know why I agreed to this, but I am sure that fond memories of Duffy played a big role. The fact that I might get a little publicity for my fledgling practice was also a factor. But this was live television! I sure didn't want to put my paw in my mouth.

The morning of the show I arrived at Dick's, where the foreboding TV remote truck sat in front of his house. I soon learned that the show was almost canceled because Barney had dug under the fence the night before and had been found only in the past hour or so, several miles from Dick's home. Shades of Duffy again. This was not going to be an easy case.

Dick did everything he could to make me feel comfortable, like going over all the questions he was going to ask me. That made me feel better at first, but when the live interview started, his first question came out of left field. I stammered, collecting my thoughts for a moment—and then I felt some dirt hit me in the face. Then a splat on my shirt. And my shoes. Dick was equally targeted.

Dick and I looked over as the TV camera panned, and we watched in amazement while Barney began excavating a rose bush right in front of us. The dirt and mud were flying, and what followed was not an interview but two full minutes of us laughing. I attempted a few token observations about why dogs like to dig, but if I did make any good points, they were literally buried as the dog's behavior took center stage.

After the commercial break, we decided we'd switch gears and talk about Barney's chewing problem. Dick went into his house and got an array of items that Barney had virtually destroyed in the previous week—items ranging from balls and Frisbees to TV remote controls to his wife's brand new high-heeled shoes and his son's stuffed animals. They weren't stuffed anymore.

As the break ended, I noticed that the cameraman seemed befuddled about something. He was waggling the wires and checking connections. "I have no audio," I heard him tell Dick.

This struck us all as odd. The previous segment had been free of any technical problems.

Sad to say, we never did do that next segment. We never did discuss why Barney loved to chew. We couldn't. Barney had chewed the microphone cord in half.

That is my memory of how I first met Dick Wolfsie. I lost touch with Dick for many years, but when Barney died I dropped him a note. Again, Barney's death had rekindled thoughts of Duffy. Dick followed up with a phone call and, as we reminisced about our first meeting, the idea for this book was born. I knew I had many humorous case studies and lots of helpful advice to share from my twenty years of treating behavior problems in dogs and cats. And I knew that Dick had a knack for telling stories in a fun and informative way.

By the way, Duffy lived to a ripe old age. At the age of twenty, I married Elaine, (my wife of forty-seven years). The beagle remained with my parents. It was my turn to leave home for a little romance of my own.

DOG BITES

Spay/neuter your dog. You want to be a responsible owner, not the godfather of the entire neighborhood canine population.

Part One
Aggression

"Money will buy a pretty good dog, but it won't buy the wag of his tail." —Josh Billings

"Do not make the mistake of treating your dogs like humans or they will treat you like dogs."
—Martha Scott

———————— Chapter 1 ————————

NOAH'S BARK

Mrs. Baxter's dog, Noah, was, to coin a phrase, a scaredy dog. Everything frightened him and sent him into a hissy-fit. The vacuum cleaner, the furnace, strangers at the front door, friends at the back door, the rattle of pans, the newspaper boy. Everything.

You name it, he was scared of it. In fact, that's all you had to do: name it. "Noah, the mailman is here." He went berserk. And thunder—thunder turned Noah into a quivering little bundle of curly black hair. He didn't know where to turn. Actually, he did. He turned to Mrs. Baxter. And there was the problem.

Now, admittedly, Noah was small. He was a toy poodle. But size does not determine a dog's courage or sensitivity to sound or threat. Some of the biggest dogs are the biggest babies. (This is true of people, too.)

To make matters worse, Noah also had more than a touch of protective aggressiveness at the front door. The dog had started nipping at people's heels when they came in, requiring Mrs. Baxter to pick Noah up to prevent him from biting. Instead of deterring this behavior, it emboldened Noah, who derived strength from his owner. "Man, she must love this yapping and nipping protection thing," he must have thought. "Why else would she pick me up?"

Next, Mrs. Baxter started putting Noah in the bedroom when the doorbell rang. *Not* a good idea. Dogs who are isolated from social interaction are perplexed by the new human scents they pick up in the house when released from their room. This confuses the dog and adds nothing to the socialization process.

Here's the bottom line: Everything Mrs. Baxter did to prevent the misbehavior was actually a motivation for Noah to continue his wayward actions. In fact, the more she tried to stop it, the worse it got. She was shaping his behavior—but not to the behavior she wanted.

As parents, we are cautioned about letting children enter our beds during a thunderstorm. We are encouraged instead to reason with them and to explain that the thunder cannot hurt them. Such soothing doesn't work with dogs. It reinforces the behavior. Even dogs that are all ears, like beagles, cannot be convinced.

One day, the dishwasher repairman was coming, so Noah was locked in the bedroom. As the repairman got on his knees to fix the broken appliance, Noah got loose and took aim at the repairman's butt, latched on for dear life, and would not let go. If you know anything about repairmen's butts, this was an easy target.

That's when I got the phone call. I soon learned from my conversation with Mrs. Baxter that she and Noah spent every waking hour together and apparently the sleeping hours, as well. Noah even ate at the dinner table in his own highchair. I'm not advocating this, just reporting it.

Like any good parent, Mrs. Baxter was protective

of her companion. When the front doorbell rang or the furnace kicked on, Mrs. Baxter picked up the yapping poodle, petted him, embraced him, coochie-cooed him, and soothed him to death. When thunder struck, she lavished him with affection. This was understandable, but a huge mistake.

It wasn't long before Noah had it all figured out. If I bark, quiver, shake, and do my Don Knotts imitation, the old lady is going to pick me up and hug me. You had to get up pretty early in the morning to fool Noah. In fact, Noah probably liked storms. After all, forty days and nights of rain was fine with his namesake.

The solution was easy. Well, easy to prescribe, but tough for Mrs. Baxter. I instructed her to ignore the dog when he barked. Do not reward or punish him. Simply pay no attention, I told her. Then I told her again. I hoped she wasn't ignoring *me*. No, she was just thinking about what I'd said.

"But what about the doorbell?" she asked. My suggestion was to give Noah a treat to stop his barking and then tie him up about six feet from the door, preventing his ankle-nipping when the guest walked in. I also instructed Mrs. Baxter to hand the "intruder" a treat to present to the dog, thus connecting the doorbell and the trespasser with positive reinforcement. Pavlov, eat your heart out.

Some people worry this approach will squelch the dog's natural instinct to be a protector. My experience convinces me that when real danger threatens, a dog instinctively knows from your demeanor (surprise/fear) and possibly from the odors you secrete in times of peril that this is for real. Any dog, even Noah, knows the difference between a burglar and a Boy Scout.

It took time, but eventually Noah learned not to overreact to every sound.

Yes, everything was fine in the end. But try to tell that to the Maytag repairman.

DOG BITES

- Picking up a small dog and holding him close to you only reinforces barking and aggression due to fear. The dog will feel supported and rewarded for his inappropriate behavior. That's exactly what you don't want.

- Your anxiety in a stressful situation can be smelled by the dog. This will accelerate his stress. You probably can't do much to prevent this, but try to relax.

- If your dog becomes anxious when the front doorbell rings, redirect his attention with treats. Make the arrival of a guest a positive experience.

- Be consistent in the tone of your voice. Use firm, clipped tones to admonish misbehaviors. A soothing tone for inappropriate behavior will reinforce that behavior.

————— **Chapter 2** —————

OSCAR THE GROUCH

You may not like hearing this, but to your dog, you are just another dog. Oh, there are differences, of course. You have two legs and you mow the lawn, but you're still a member of the pack. The top dog, but still a dog.

Maintaining your position as leader of the pack is usually not that tough. After all, you are the walker and the feeder, and you probably tower over your canine pal. (If the dog is number one in your house, you *really* need this book.)

When there is a change in the dynamics of the pack, there can be some jockeying for position. A new girlfriend or boyfriend, a stray cat, or another dog can upset the order of things. Generally, this is more of a distraction than a major problem, but there are exceptions.

Oscar was one of those exceptions. The problem we had with Oscar had some dangerous implications. And it's a story I had heard too many times before.

Oscar was a three-year-old pug, happily submissive to his owners, Mr. and Mrs. Yacobson, but quite pleased with his dominance over Max, a ninety-pound Lab who was a big dufus and probably enjoyed being pushed around. Even though Oscar was number three in the pack, he was treated very well, often sleeping on the bed with the Yacobsons or resting in their laps.

Enter Maggie. Not another big lovable Lab that Oscar could control, but an adorable little baby girl who turned Oscar's world upside down. Oscar wanted to stay number three. That's where the problem began.

For the first year, a newborn like Maggie does not usually create a problem. The dog may feel a loss of attention, but because the child must either be held by Mom or Dad or kept in the crib, there is little opportunity for a dog protecting his place in the pack to do anything that would pose a risk to the child.

But toddlers are another issue. As Maggie matured and began to walk, she was eyeball-to-eyeball with Oscar. Her rough petting and occasional falling on him unnerved Oscar. Combine this with his gradual recognition that she threatened his status in the house, and it led to growling when Maggie came close to him, which led to a phone call to me.

Oscar needed a demotion. Having been neutered, you'd have thought he was accustomed to a little humiliation, but it was time to get Oscar off the furniture and off the bed. After all, Maggie slept in a crib in her own room. So step one was to make Oscar realize that he was not a rank above the baby. In fact, he was not above anything on two legs, even if Maggie was crawling. That meant sleeping in the laundry room with Max. No more sharing a bed with number one and number two. Poor Oscar! But it was a necessary step. Oscar was going to be number four, whether he liked it or not.

I asked that Oscar be kept on a six-foot-long lead in the house to allow the Yacobsons to have direct control over him at all times. In addition, the Yacobsons gave him constant commands, like COME, SIT, STAY! Or COME, DOWN, STAY! This way, Oscar was further reminded they were the alphas, the top dogs. Every time the dog obeys a command, it's submissive to the owner and the owner becomes more dominant. And just to add a little more reinforcement, I told the Yacobsons to hold Maggie when they gave commands. I wanted Maggie to start looking like a number three to Oscar.

I also did not want Oscar practicing his dominance or aggression with anyone. Even Max. If Oscar demonstrated aggressive traits in any context, he was reprimanded and given a fifteen-minute time-out in the bathroom.

Oscar wasn't the only one who needed a little training. I always recommend to new parents that they instruct toddlers in the proper way to treat the family pet. No ear tugging, no tail pulling. Just gentle strokes on the neck and shoulders. And most important, I strongly suggest to parents that small children not carry food around the house in the dog's presence or feed him treats. The dog begins to think that all food at his level is for him, and this can result in the dog attempting to steal the food, which can lead to a bite, although it may be inadvertent.

I told Mr. and Mrs. Y. that whenever they saw Maggie approach Oscar, they were to call Oscar and give him a treat if he did not growl at Maggie, thus teaching Oscar that avoiding the child had some benefits. This rewards Oscar for not interacting with the child alone and reinforces the COME command. It also rewards Oscar for not controlling his space by growling and trying to chase Maggie away.

In addition, we orchestrated upbeat playtime for the entire family that was structured so Maggie could pet and be close to Oscar while Mr. and Mrs. Y. offered treats. It would be a positive experience for both.

Oscar soon learned to avoid Maggie and came running to the Yacobsons for treats when Maggie came close. He quickly accepted the fact that another two-legged dog to whom he needed to be subservient was in the house, too. He still pushed Max around a little, but Max was happy being number five. He never aspired to anything else. Max just wasn't cut out for middle management.

DOG BITES

- Every time your dog obeys your command, this reinforces that you are dominant and he subservient. Give commands often. Command him to do things he is not doing. When he's sitting, tell him to lay down. When he's laying down, tell him to sit.

- The most effective time-out room is a room the dog is not familiar with. Time-out is not a vacation. It's a temporary separation from his entertaining world and an isolation from his pack.

• Children under the age of three (usually at eye level with the pooch) should not give treats to the dog. The dog cannot distinguish whose food it is. The dog might become a food stealer, often frightening and possibly hurting the child.

• If you want your dog to feel comfortable around a new baby, make sure good things happen when the baby is around by providing treats and giving toys to play with.

• Teach your dog to come to you when the baby is crawling around unsupervised by offering the dog a treat. This way, you are rewarding your dog for avoiding the baby.

—————— Chapter 3 ——————

Q.E. LOUIE

Sometimes, otherwise well-behaved dogs develop a less-than-friendly attitude around mealtime. Louie was a good example of a food-aggressive dog. The four-year-old Jack Russell terrier was a rescued dog, and he had spent a good part of his life either as a stray or at the pound, where he probably had to fight for or protect his food. Louie was also a food stealer. No counter was too high, no garbage pail too secure, no hand with food safe from his tiny jaws. To make matters worse, he was actually beginning to growl at his owners, Mr. and Mrs. Warren, if they entered his "space" while he was eating from his bowl.

Growling at a family member is a huge red flag. But the Warrens had been considering a call even before that started. They had been planning a trip to Europe for the summer and looked forward to traveling with Louie. Europe, as you probably know, is much more accommodating to people with pets, allowing dogs to sit under tables or beside their masters in restaurants and cafes. But Louie's table manners and his possessiveness were sources of concern. And in Paris, where French poodles look down on English terriers anyway, Louie needed to be on his best behavior.

After my initial conversation with the Warrens, I instructed them to keep Louie out of the kitchen. Early in the reconditioning process, it is important not to set a dog up to fail. Later in the training, temptation can be used to further strengthen the learning process, but at first we do not want the dog to experience any unnecessary inducements to misbehave.

I told the Warrens to use toys to help teach the word GIVE. When Louie had a toy in his mouth, he learned that by releasing his possession at the command GIVE! he would be rewarded with a treat. Once the word GIVE had been learned, that conditioning could be transferred more easily to the food problem.

Within a few weeks, Louie was allowed to return the kitchen, but counters were cleared and garbage pails were hidden away. Louie was directed to sit/stay or lay/stay on his pillow to further drive home the fact that the Warrens were in charge, especially in the kitchen. Initially, we tied his leash to a doorknob so that he would not even attempt to scavenge for food anywhere in the room. The kitchen was slowly losing its allure.

The Warrens also had Louie sit as they hand-fed food pellets to him from his bowl, reinforcing the fact that if Louie was overly aggressive, the feeding was stopped. If he was compliant, the food was kicked up a notch in flavor—from biscuit to bratwurst, for example. The Warrens were reminding Louie that while they were in control of the food, Louie could favorably affect his own situation by responding appropriately.

The Warrens began a feeding routine where they instructed Louie to sit, then held the bowl in their hands while Louie ate and sporadically gave the command GIVE. The bowl was then taken away. If Louie growled, the Warrens would say NO, stop feeding, and withhold the bowl of food until fifteen minutes later. But if Louie did not respond aggressively, he immediately got his food back with a nice chunk of pepperoni on top. Louie caught on fast: "Hey, I'll let them take the bowl. I'm even better off when I get it back." This soon allowed them to feed him on the floor and remove it without his growling.

The Warrens were superb clients, dedicated to changing Louie's behavior—and they were psyched for their trip to Europe on the Queen Elizabeth. They set sail early that summer and were pleased with the rehabilitated Louie.

Just three days into the trip, a call came to my office. It was a conference call from the Q.E. 2. On the phone were the ship's captain, Louie's regular veterinarian calling from his office in town, and the Warrens. This was not a good sign. I knew it wasn't a thank-you call.

Louie had been a bad boy. Because he had to stay in the ship's kennel for much of the trip, he became overly stressed. His conditioning process at home had been specific to his familiar surroundings and his owners. The new living arrangements confused him, and he reverted to his old behavior. In plain English: Louie took a bite out of the fleshy part of the kennel worker's leg while being fed.

We discussed the problem, but there were not many options available for Louie. The Warrens were frequent sailors and had a little pull with the captain, so Louie was allowed to stay in the stateroom instead of the kennel. And he was permitted to use the balcony for relief as long as the Warrens were diligent in cleaning up. This honor of a canine companion being permitted to stay in a guest's stateroom had been bestowed only once before on this ship—and that was for Rufus, the faithful canine companion of Winston Churchill.

The first night Louie stayed in the stateroom, the Warrens went to dinner on the ship. Everyone in line was pushing and shoving to get to the head of the buffet. Passengers grumbled when the kitchen ran out of the jumbo prawns, and two women fought over the last chocolate éclair.

But Louie had to stay in his room. After all, he was food aggressive.

Oh, by the way, I got a Christmas card from Louie that December.

"Thanks a lot," said the note. "You did a good job changing my parents' behavior."

Author's note: Louie returned to America not on the Q.E. 2, but in a two-thousand-dollar seat on the Concorde. Mr. and Mrs. Warren were taking no chances that Louie might not be well-mannered on the long return trip at sea. Louie enjoyed the plane ride. Why not? He sat next to Mr. Warren and Mrs. Warren had to sit behind Louie. But he was a perfect gentleman. Rumor has it that even when the opportunity presented itself, Louie did not eat the last peanut.

DOG BITES

- Set your dog up to win. Put him in situations where you can reward him. Avoid situations where he would be admonished.

- Teach your dog to GIVE or DROP his favorite toy. This is another way to reinforce your dominance. If your dog becomes a "stealer," you'll be glad you taught him this command.

——————— **Chapter 4** ———————

HOUNDED BY A BEAGLE

Mr. and Mrs. Hetherington were perplexed as to why their new four-month-old beagle puppy, Toby, wasn't more like Ben, their fifteen-year-old Lab that had recently died. Ben was a faithful companion that lived to a ripe old age, despite being withered by arthritis.

Over the years, I have heard this lament a great deal. People lose a beloved pet, then replace him. But they conveniently forget what their old dog was like when he was a puppy—assuming they even had him when he was a puppy. In this way pet owners are like mothers who often forget about the "terrible twos." That's why many people have younger brothers and sisters.

Without researching the differences, the Hetheringtons had replaced their Lab with a beagle, which is kind of like replacing Mr. Rogers with Jim Carrey. Beagles are a high-energy breed, always into mischief and looking for treats.

Nevertheless, the Hetheringtons had chosen a beagle. And he was smart as a whip. I have a saying that a tired dog is a good dog. Now I say this: A dumb dog is a good dog. Why? Because smart dogs like Toby are always one step ahead of their owners. Leave a top off the garbage, they're waiting. Take your socks off before retiring, there's the beagle at the bedroom door waiting for a new "toy." Smart dogs like Toby know how to work the system.

Mr. and Mrs. Hetherington were in their early seventies and both still worked, which meant leaving Toby in his crate all day. After nine hours in a crate, a beagle pup is ready to party and he'd come bounding out of his "den" with more energy than they could really handle. Let the games begin. Toby got in the garbage, jumped up on the table, stole laundry out of the bin. He was hell on wheels. And he didn't want to spend any time outside. His family (pack)—and all the action—was inside.

Toby didn't have a mean bone in his body, but his method of play was too feisty for his own good. First, he was mouthy. When the Hetheringtons played with him, he nipped, lightly to be sure, but the result was some pretty nicked up arms, hands, and fingers. Toby's exuberance frightened the couple.

In order to nip this nipping in the bud, Mr. Hetherington decided to punish the dog when he felt Toby was being too rough. So almost every day Toby was being yelled at, struck on the rump with a hand or newspaper, and even hit with a fly swatter. Mr. Hetherington was a fan of the old school of discipline, but he was really making matters worse. Instead of squashing the inappropriate responses, he was escalating their frequency and intensity. Toby would be punished for being a bit testy and then, as a result of the punishment, he would act up even more. This is called a vicious cycle, and it had started to make Toby aggressive, causing growling, snarling, and snapping at the fly swatter and newspaper.

Most pups in a litter will test the limits of their aggressive playing. Dogs know that a squeal from a littermate means: "Your roughhousing has gone too far. I don't want to play anymore." Toby had lost this sensitivity as a result of the way his misbehavior was being managed. His owners' behavior only escalated his aggression.

In our first phone call, I told the couple we needed to set up Toby to win by limiting where he could wander in the house. He had far too many rooms for mischief, so we restricted him to the living room and kitchen by using baby gates and closed doors. I also suggested (as I often do) a six-foot cord be attached to Toby's collar so they had total control of him in the house. If they were watching TV, for example, he would be tied to the leg of the chair or couch next to them, and during this time they would give him toys and reward him with treats. And even if he were loose in the kitchen or dining room, the lead would remain dragging from his collar, a reminder that he was under their control. If he jumped on the table or stole food from the trash, it was easier to stop him. Two seventy-year-olds should not be chasing a beagle around the house. Actually, it's impossible for two seventy-year-olds to chase a beagle around the house.

The cord also allowed the Hetheringtons to constantly issue obedience commands to Toby like COME, SIT, STAY. Or COME, DOWN, STAY. They could enforce the command with the cord and reinforce it with treats. This was further evidence to the beagle that he was third in the pack order and that the arrangement wasn't going to change. It reached the point fairly quickly that Toby wanted to submit to a command because it usually meant a piece of kibble. After all, he was a beagle.

Most important, the Hetheringtons were to dispense with all physical punishment or threat of it. No fly swatters, no rolled up newspapers. And definitely no striking with the hand, or physical play, no matter how softly. We wanted to keep the hand a positive symbol, a symbol of gentle strokes to come or, even better, of a treat given.

I have always said that if a beagle doesn't want a treat, he's sick. And Toby, a credit to his breed, was a treat freak. That was the saving grace of their beagle selection. It would make it easier to shape his behavior.

The Hetheringtons also armed themselves with a water bottle and gave Toby a healthy squirt whenever his behavior was starting to become physical. If Toby became mouthy, they were also to utter "ouch" and squirt him. This was an indication to Toby that he had gone too far in his play. Following the rough interaction, Toby was to be tied away from his owners for ten minutes. For most dogs, and especially beagles who love attention, that hurts more than a fly swatter.

And we needed to tire that dog out. Lots of walks and play with toys. It usually helps. It never hurts.

The Hetheringtons followed my instructions to a tee. And Toby was a typical hound, in love with anything that would fit in his mouth. This was a winning combination for shaping behavior, and it led to a happy ending.

Toby stopped his nipping and snarling, but make no mistake, he did not become a perfect angel. He was, after all, still a beagle.

DOG BITES

- A smart dog is usually more trouble than a dumb dog. A smart dog is always a step ahead of you.

- Don't roughhouse or play tug-o-war with an already aggressive dog. It will make things worse.

- You can shape a beagle's behavior with treats. If treats don't work, then either you need a better treat or it's not a beagle.

—————— **Chapter 5** ——————

THE HAND THAT FEEDS YOU

When Mr. Herkimer called and said that he and his wife were having problems in the bedroom, it was enough to make a middle-aged veterinarian blush.

It wasn't the first time I had heard this story. The Herkimers' two-year-old German shepherd, Bonnie, had taken a bite out of Mr. Herkimer's left arm while he and his wife were retiring the previous night. Mr. Herkimer referred to Bonnie as a Dr. Jekyll and Mr. Hyde.

He used his right arm to call me. He was correct to do so. When a dog bites the hand that feeds her, the problem has usually been building for a while. In this case, Mr. Herkimer's routine each evening had been reinforcing the problem. Mr. H. often went to bed after his wife and Bonnie had retired. When he got ready to go to bed, he'd toss a bisuit on the floor to coax Bonnie to move away from Mrs. H's side. Then Mr. H. would jump into bed and pull the covers over his head.

Then that fateful night, the timing was a little off: A premature toss of the biscuit and a late arrival under the covers, and Mr. Herkimer was nailed by a shiny set of canines.

This was just one way that the Herkimers had

unknowingly enabled this situation by reinforcing the dog's evolving determination to become the alpha of the family pack.

Bonnie had always been a bit feisty, growling or showing her teeth with an occasional air snap if she was challenged or provoked. Mr. Herkimer would ignore Bonnie if he sensed the dog was being a touch aggressive toward him. Mrs. Herkimer often compounded the problem by stroking Bonnie and talking lovingly to calm her after she had exhibited this inappropriate behavior. These behaviors by the Herkimers reinforced Bonnie's dominance.

Rewarding Bonnie's demeanor just escalated the problem, and ultimately Bonnie became protective and controlling of Mrs. Herkimer, convinced that this guardian role afforded her some benefit and strengthened her position in the pack as number one. Slowly but surly, Bonnie's behavior escalated from grumbling to growling and then to snapping. Bonnie was upping the ante.

Further proof of her developing sense of dominance was that Bonnie also became possessive and a stealer: Socks, TV remotes, and eyeglasses vanished. She became protective of her sleeping areas like the sofa and the big family chair, growling when Mr. or Mrs. H. approached. Bonnie was showing her muscle by protecting her resources. Mrs. H. was a pushover. She never admonished Bonnie, and she had a soft soothing voice. She was also the primary feeder. Mrs. H. had value to Bonnie, and was therefore seen as a resource. In Bonnie's eyes, Mrs. H. needed to be protected from her husband.

The result of all this was the ultimate insult to any dog owner: being bitten by your own pet. Both humiliating and frightening.

And to make the situation even more exasperating, Bonnie was pretty much a perfect lady with other people. In fact, she was downright friendly with house guests and people she met on walks. It seemed as though she had saved most of her wrath for Mr. Herkimer, the guy who most often played with and walked her. Talk about gratitude!

The shepherd needed an attitude adjustment. Her role in the family had clearly climbed, and Bonnie saw herself as the alpha of the pack, ahead of her owners. To challenge that status she first needed to be stripped of all the trappings of superiority. That meant being controlled.

Bonnie was about to become attached to a new friend— a six-foot-long nylon cord tied to her collar that she would drag around the house to serve as a reminder that she was controlled by the Herkimers. She was no longer a free spirit. They could use the cord to make Bonnie come and obey other orders and to dissuade her from any inappropriate behavior. The cord was their control line.

The Herkimers were to pepper each day with cord-controlled commands such as COME, DOWN, STAY and COME, SIT, STAY, frequent reminders that she was not the CEO, not the alpha of this small pack. But while I wanted the Herkimers to constantly show Bonnie they were boss, I did not want Bonnie in situations that would set her up for failure. In conjunction with this, Bonnie was taught the word DROP, so that if she was caught stealing the TV remote, she would submit it immediately. This is hard to teach most husbands.

The ideal situation was to keep her out of bedrooms where she could sleep on beds, and when she found a resting place on a sofa or chair, she was immediately taken by the cord and marched into the bathroom for time-out. No more sleeping on the bed or napping on the furniture. Height is power and dominance, and Bonnie was going to have to lower her sights.

After fifteen minutes of solitude in the time-out room, she was let out, given a command to sit or lay down, and then released. The Herkimers were to ignore her for a half-hour afterward. Time-out is a very effective punishment for a dog that thinks it is in control.

It was clear that Bonnie should not be harshly admonished or threatened, since both responses would only heighten her aggression toward the Herkimers.

When Bonnie came for attention or to be petted, the Herkimers were to go through a few basic commands first. Bonnie needed to know there was no free love. Affection was to be on the Herkimers' terms. If she wanted something, she first had to demonstrate submissiveness.

When she went out of the house, she was commanded to SIT and then to follow Mr. or Mrs. H. instead of leading. Bonnie was to sit or lay down and stay before receiving her food. If she did not finish the food, it was taken away. The Herkimers needed to make a statement that they controlled the valuable resource of food. Nothing in Bonnie's life was to lead her to think she was the top dog. Even her toys were controlled. They were given to her to play with but taken away when playtime was over.

This was a slow process. Bonnie's rise to power had been gradual, and her fall would also take time. As always, I suggested that the cord remain on at all times, although I was comfortable with them shortening it as her submissiveness increased and its use became infrequent.

Sensing this weight on her collar and occasionally directing her with it was a constant reminder that she was no longer in control.

Last I heard, there was no more growling in the bedroom. At least not from Bonnie.

DOG BITES

- When commanding a dog, use a firm, confident tone. Do not threaten. Do not raise your voice. Speak as you'd like to be spoken to by your boss.

- You can reinforce a dog's submissiveness (and your dominance) by issuing commands just for the heck of it. Sounds silly, but it works.

- Don't let your dog play the "now you may pet me" game. When your pooch wants a little attention, give it on your terms by first requiring that he obey a simple command.

• A six-foot cord (or control line) attached to your dog's collar in the house will remind him that he is being controlled. But be sure not to leave a cord on an unattended dog.

• If your dog has bitten, he may bite again under similar circumstances. Proper behavior management can reduce the chances it will happen again. But be careful!

———— Chapter 6 ————

DUTCH TREATS

Life out West was pretty good for Dutch, the Kiestersons' three-year-old boxer. Dutch hung out most of the day enjoying the beautiful Arizona weather, lounging in the backyard, soaking up rays and chewing his rawhide bone. But Dutch didn't know what he was missing. Literally. His life was spent entirely behind a privacy fence, isolated from the normal hustle and bustle of daily life. No other dogs, no kids, no nothing.

Things were about to change for Dutch. He was going to get a sudden dose of reality. The Kiestersons were moving to Indianapolis. And the new home did not have a privacy fence; it had a chainlink fence surrounding the whole yard.

Dutch was unprepared for the stimulation. Suddenly the world looked like Dr. Seuss's *And to Think That I Saw It on Mulberry Street,* just one exciting challenge after another: mailmen, ambulances, kids on tricycles, FedEx trucks, joggers, skateboarders. HELLO WORLD!

Well, you can take the dog out of Arizona, but you can't take the instinct out of the dog. Dutch wanted attention, and he also wanted to guard his new home from these potential intruders. Like a sentry, he paced the fence, barking at all who passed. And the most amazing things happened: Whenever he barked at the FedEx truck, it disappeared. And when he barked at a skateboarder, he was gone in seconds. And that ambulance? Well, one bark from Dutch and it was now three blocks away. After a couple of weeks of this, Dutch was getting a loud and clear message: HEY, I AM REALLY GOOD AT THIS WATCHDOG THING.

This is a common scenario. The dog sees results for barking, and this reinforces the bad behavior. Years ago, dogs barked at the milkmen. There are no milkmen anymore. Dogs have taken credit for this.

Dutch's new demeanor resulted in a different behavior toward guests inside the house, as well. He saw himself for the first time as a protector and actually became aggressive. It was a side of Dutch the Kiestersons had never seen. And they didn't like it. In fact, it frightened them.

When I spoke with the Kiestersons, I made it very clear that they were going to have to make a real commitment to changing Dutch's thinking. I do not pay visits to people's homes, because I am not the one who modifies the pet's behavior. The owners do this. I told the Kiestersons I hoped they had a lovely yard because they were going to have to spend some serious time there. The reason is simple: Dutch needed to be corrected immediately for inappropriate behavior. You couldn't leave Dutch out all day to bark, then come home and discipline him for what seemed to him to have been working fine all day. That is setting a dog up for failure.

I wanted the Kiestersons to reinforce their dominance over Dutch. I told them to frequently make him respond to commands like SIT/STAY and DOWN/STAY. A dog needs a strong pack leader. And reestablishing this was important so that their commands to him would be heeded both inside and outside of the house.

We began by not letting Dutch in the yard alone. When he was there, he was attached to a long lead so if he barked at someone he could be caught by his owners and silenced quickly. QUIET! they would say. In addition, Dutch was taken on long walks, exposing him to people outside the yard who would give him treats if he quieted down and sat on command. Dutch was neither hard of hearing nor stupid. He caught on pretty quickly.

Later on, when Dutch was alone in the yard, I encouraged the Kiestersons to get the word out in the neighborhood that if Dutch made a fuss when anyone passed the fence, it was okay to come over and interact with him. The neighborhood kids, upon hearing Dutch bark, began gravitating toward the chainlink fence, where I suggested a metal container containing biscuits be attached so kids could throw treats into the yard. Dutch was beginning to think this protection thing was not all it was cracked up to be.

Dutch made significant progress, but to move things along a bit more quickly, I suggested that the Kiestersons build a privacy fence in part of the backyard so Dutch could be unattended without the stimulation, just like in Arizona.

This was a classic case where the pet owner had to make a commitment to replace the dog's bad behavior with a good one. There is no magic wand, just hard work—although a pocketful of Pupperoni strips given by others can be very helpful.

Dutch soon chilled out and enjoy a quiet life in the

yard, although he is considering moving back to Arizona when he retires. Winter in Indiana can be tough. Even on a dog.

DOG BITES

- Always walk a dog toward traffic. Dogs prefer to see what's coming toward them. Sounds and images popping up from behind can cause anxiety.

- A treat should not be a bribe. Have your dog obey your command, then provide a treat with praise as a reinforcer.

- Don't forget to praise your dog for good behavior. It works, and it's never fattening.

- Fences don't make for good neighbors or good dogs. Fences can instill protective and aggressive behaviors in dogs if the dog is left unattended frequently for long periods.

- Every dog is different. Every human is different. That's why every interaction between pooch and person can be somewhat unpredictable.

Chapter 7

GOLDEN YEARS

Benny and Rex were buddies. The two golden Labs played together, ate together, and were walked together. They were Lab partners.

Roger Johnson, their owner, was engaged to Jennifer, a lovely young lady who was crazy about the dogs as well. There had been considerable movement back and forth between the two apartments during the courtship, and the dogs seemed to cope pretty well. They enjoyed both residences and, like Roger, had grown to love Jennifer.

The fairy tale ended when Jennifer and Roger got married. I think I had better explain that.

Once the happy couple moved in together, Benny went though a strange transformation. He became possessive of his toys, snapping at his buddy Rex when the other Lab wanted to play. Benny became assertive and barked uncontrollably when Roger and Jennifer were affectionate with one another. Since they were still on their honeymoon, the dog didn't have many good days. On more than one occasion, Benny growled at Jennifer. I am sure that being newlyweds, Roger growled a bit at Jennifer, as well, but that was understandable.

Rex, by the way, had no problem with the affection. He

just sat there and watched. Whatever makes you happy.

This controlling dominant behavior toward Jennifer troubled the couple. Their call to me was one of desperation. They felt almost guilty. Had they done anything to cause this? YES, I told them. You got married.

"HUH?"

I explained that in all dog packs there is a kind of pecking order, an unfortunate metaphor because it refers to chickens, which I refuse to treat—even pet chickens.

In this case, the two dogs had been comfortable with the previous arrangement. Roger was clearly number one, the alpha, if you will. And Benny was a clear second. Rex was third, but the dynamics were such that Benny and Rex seldom squabbled. Everyone was comfortable with the hierarchy.

After the marriage, there was a huge shift in the dynamics. While Roger and Jennifer might have disagreed on who between them the ruled the roost (darn, another chicken metaphor), it was pretty clear to Benny that he was now number three. No one likes a demotion. Benny was unhappy.

Because Benny's position in the pack had been compromised, he had to overcompensate and show Rex for the first time that he was the boss. Rex had always known Benny was the boss, but for the first time, Benny was rubbing it in. This behavior is rooted in tens of thousands of years of living in packs—family groups that required social structure and order.

At this point, it was important *not* to reinforce Benny's new habits. Benny was looking for feedback for his show of dominance, and I suggested they not give it. Instead, I encouraged Roger to distance himself from Benny.

He could acknowledge and occasionally pet him—that was okay—but I cautioned Roger about encouraging any of Benny's overprotectiveness of him and Benny's dominance of Jennifer.

I proposed a program to squelch that dominance. I suggested that Jennifer feed Benny every night, a move that combined two positive results: It reinforced the fact that Jennifer was dominant (she controlled his food and his toys), but it also created a positive relationship between Benny and the newest heir to the throne. To further augment this idea, we kept Benny on a six-foot lead, controlled by Jennifer, again reinforcing the fact that she was the boss. She also walked him and rewarded him with treats when he periodically obeyed her commands of COME, SIT/STAY, and DOWN/STAY.

What was happening is not too different from what happens in human relationships (which I know a bit more about than chickens). There is always some juggling for superiority in any association, but often members of the group willingly and happily accept the inferior role. It works. There's something in it for them *not* to be the boss.

That's what was happening with Benny. It was clear that Jennifer was going to share top role with Roger. But what the heck. Benny was getting two squares a day, lots of treats, and great tummy rubs. Being number three could have been worse.

The key, of course, is that Jennifer exercised control in a positive way. And she managed to orchestrate things so that Benny remained dominant over Rex. Going from number two to number three was acceptable, but going to number four would have been, well, humiliating (in an evolutionary sense).

After a few weeks, the Johnsons were a big happy family. Benny no longer picked on Rex because he was comfortable in his new role. And Jennifer and Benny had become inseparable. In fact, she had to uninvite Benny when going to the bathroom. Jennifer became Benny's primary caretaker and spent much of her free time with him on walks and playing.

Now Roger felt *he* wasn't getting enough attention. That's when I got another phone call.

Sorry, I don't do wives, husbands, and kids.

DOG BITES

- Dogs respond best to words. Avoid phrases. Full sentences? Don't even bother.

- Intermittently reinforcing a dog with treats results in anticipation, which will develop a stronger response than giving a treat every time.

- When you begin training your dog, hold the treat up to your face to get your dog's attention. Make eye contact and give the command.

- If the pack make-up changes (with the loss or gain of animals or people) expect a readjustment to occur. Everyone will be jockeying for position.

- Once training has progressed, first have the dog respond to your command. Then reveal and give the treat. This makes the treat a reinforcer, not a bribe.

Chapter 8

DOING IT TO THE MAX

Shultz was a seventy-five-pound husky/shepherd/rottweiler blend. Max was a twenty-pound cocker spaniel. You'll never guess who thought he was boss.

Wow! You *did* guess it. Of course, if Max didn't think *he* was the boss, this wouldn't be a very interesting story.

There were a lot of reasons Max thought he was on top. He had been Mrs. Beinstock's "Little Muffin" for eight years. Shultz was a more recent acquisition, a rescue from the local humane society. Being a small dog, Max spent much of the day in Mrs. Beinstock's lap while she was sitting in her rocking chair and crocheting.

Max and Shultz did okay when they were out in the yard together, but inside the house Max became very protective of his relationship with Mrs. B. When Shultz approached his mistress while she was fawning over Max, the cocker's lip would quiver, then a little snarl would erupt. Mrs. B would then bend down, talk softly, and try to calm him.

At first Mrs. B. was tickled, flattered that Max was showing his love for her by being protective of their bond. Shultz wasn't tickled; he was ticked. Shultz was not an aggressive dog by nature, but he was all alpha and he didn't like being growled at by a dog not only fifty pounds lighter, but pretty much devoid of any other leadership qualities that make one dog superior over another dog in the pack.

The result was at least two fights between the dogs, including one that knocked the old lady and her cocker off their rocker and scared Mrs. B. to death. Mrs. B. broke up the skirmish, but the event was so unsettling that I could barely understand her on the phone.

The problem, of course, was Mrs. B. herself. She felt a strong obligation toward Max and in both overt and subtle ways, making and maintaining Max as the top dog. This was a big mistake. Max was never going to be the alpha.

"But Dr. Sampson, he was here first. Shouldn't he be number one?"

This is an assumption that many pet owners make when they add a dog to the family. They either take for granted that the first dog is the alpha or that the bigger dog will be dominant. Neither assumption is necessarily correct. The alpha quality is genetic. It's difficult to modify, and Mrs. B. was not the kind of person equipped to alter the natural order of things. She herself was barely a beta, even on her best day.

The challenge in this case was to establish Shultz's position in the family without creating a monster. Shultz already knew he was boss, but Max needed a little education in this area. And we needed Mrs. B.'s help.

First, no more lap time for Max. Sitting in Mrs. B.'s lap was giving him a false sense of status by virtue of height. Max was also kept off all furniture, including the bed. In addition, Max was always to be fed after Shultz. At the back door, Shultz was to exit first, and upon return, Shultz would lead the way back into the house. Shultz was to be first in everything.

If Mrs. B. was petting Max and Shultz walked over, I instructed her to ignore Max and pay immediate attention to Shultz. If Mrs. B. was petting Shultz first, she was to ignore Max if he tried to horn in. Later, she could gently acknowledge him. Max still needed to be loved. But he was number two.

Unlike a kids' fight that requires some detective work to identify the instigator, in the case of a Max-Shultz bout, the assumption was to be made that Max set Shultz up and was the cause, sending the cocker to time-out (a bathroom or laundry room devoid of toys or the dog's bed). Message to Max: When you battle an alpha, you lose. Shultz is the alpha of the dog pack.

Yes, Shultz was the alpha, but we did not want this idea to go to his head. We wanted Shultz to be a sweet loveable alpha, a kind of benevolent dictator. And we wanted Mrs. B. to still be number one of the total pack, a position she had only tenuously held onto during all these tense times.

To assert her dominance, Mrs. B. made sure that Shultz was repeatedly given commands throughout the day: COME! SIT/STAY. DOWN/STAY. Such repetition confirmed Shultz's subservience to his caretaker. These commands could be given at random, but they were *always* to be used when Shultz approached Mrs. B. for attention. This was also done with Max, but only after working with Shultz.

When dogs approach you to garner attention, they are usually saying, "You may pet me now on my terms."

By immediately barking orders, so to speak, you can maintain your superiority. Command the dog to take a new position: SIT or DOWN. You are saying to the dog: I will be happy to pet you, but on my terms. There is no free love.

The process with Max and Shultz took awhile. It is tough for an owner who doesn't realize this hierarchy thing is not something you can adjust based on your personal feelings about your dogs.

Max had risen to a position he was not comfortable with. Once off his lofty perch, (Mrs. B.'s lap and bed), he soon accepted second position and became less testy toward Shultz, even eliciting play with him. It soon became obvious that Max liked having Shultz as his leader and protector when meeting strangers or other dogs in the park. Shultz always led the way, and Max followed. Max had been in over his head, and now he knew it.

Mrs. B. had learned the hard way: It's not nice (or wise) to mess with Mother Nature.

DOG BITES

- When your dog comes for attention, he is actually granting you permission to pet him. Don't let him call the shots. Issue a command first; then interact with him.

- Why do dogs sometimes fight with each other? To be alpha dogs and control resources of food, toys, space, and the owner's attention.

- Some dogs aspire to a higher ranking in the pack. Frequent commands to obey you will stifle that and reinforce your dominance.

- Height is power and dominance like the throne of a monarch. A dog that is permitted to sit on beds, couches and chairs may start to think he is king. Or queen. Keep dogs on the floor.

- When adding a second dog to your family/pack, consider opposite sexes. Same sexes have a higher frequency of fighting.

Chapter 9

PUPPYGATE

Over the years, I have been called as an expert witness in a few legal cases involving incidents where someone was injured by another person's pet and then looked to put the bite on the pet owner—financially.

I have worked with both plaintiffs and defendants; however, most of the time I am on the side of the animal and its owner. My role is to explain why the animal behaved in that manner, to establish whether it was (or was not) vicious, and to determine whether the attack may have been provoked. Such testimony helps establish appropriate damages. Since insurance companies are usually represented by both sides, hefty awards loom as a possibility. I've seen them go as high as $250,000.

I have assisted in jury selection, always hoping to find pet owners, who usually are more understanding of an animals' needs and instincts. And women are usually better jurors for the defense, often being even more sensitive to the animal's issues. I have also assisted lawyers in developing questions for depositions, which elicit information that will be helpful to the jury. In many instances, the case never reaches trial.

Most cases involve an animal bite. Cat bite cases

are relatively rare, but when they occur they can be dangerous. Cat bites are really inoculations. The pin-like teeth can imbed the bacteria from the cat's mouth deep into the skin. Dog bites appear more dangerous on the surface, but in reality the bite may flush itself out due to the bleeding. All animal bites must be taken seriously, but do not underestimate the seriousness of a cat bite.

Sometimes the most harmful aspect of an animal bite is when the incident affects the relationships between friends and families. Many dog bites occur when a dog comes in contact with an unfamiliar person. If the dog is unfriendly or has an aggressive demeanor, this can lead to an inappropriate response to a stranger—sometimes a provoked response, sometimes not. But some bites occur when good people and good dogs find themselves in an awkward situation. That was the case with the Brown family and the Bufords.

The Browns' dog, Terri, was a three-year-old terrier who was a hit with all the kids who knew her. Not only was she friendly, but her recent litter of pups had caused quite a stir. In fact, many of the youngsters in the neighborhood had witnessed the birth of Comet, Donner, Blitzen, and Rudolph (it was Christmastime).

Terri and her pups found privacy behind a baby gate attached to the laundry room doorway, but Terri seemed to enjoy the frequent parade of adults and kids who came over to see and play with the tiny terriers, as their eyes opened and they sought attention and handling. Does a mother dog feel pride for her litter? If you had seen Terri, you'd have little question.

One day while Mrs. Brown and Mrs. Buford were chatting over coffee at the Browns' home, they failed to keep a watchful eye on Mrs. Buford's daughter, Sarah, the two-year-old princess who made her way to the laundry room to see Terri and her puppies. Sarah leaned in on the gate just a wee bit too much, and the wooden protector came crashing to the floor, trapping all of Rudolph and half of Comet in the chaos. Mrs. Buford and Mrs. Brown heard the thud of the gate and the high-pitched squealing of the puppies. They reacted quickly, but not as quickly as Terri. Mama dog's response to the crying dogs was immediate. She saw the commotion as a threat and took a small chunk out of Sarah's face as soon as the frightened little girl hit the laundry room floor.

Never were so many so frightened for so many different reasons. Sarah was rushed to the hospital for emergency treatment. It was the beginning of a trial of the friendship between Mrs. Brown and Mrs. Buford and the beginning of a long recuperative process for Sarah, both medically and emotionally.

This is such a sad case because even the most casual observer would recognize that the attack was provoked, albeit not intentionally. Terri's response to protect her puppies was an instinct. Humans will react as quickly to protect their young.

In this case, I was asked by the Browns' insurance company to testify to the circumstances that caused the bite. The Bufords' lawyers wanted a settlement not just for medical bills, but for pain and suffering—some compensation for the years of plastic surgery that Sarah faced.

I make no claim to having any insight into how much payment for damages was appropriate, what constituted a legitimate settlement, or what the lawyers deserved. Based on what I came to learn about the case, however, I was at least initially pretty certain this dog's attack was an isolated and understandable response to what happened.

But a gut response is not enough. Knowing I would be deposed, I needed to provide stronger proof (not just an opinion) that the dog was a sweetheart. In preparation for the case, I gave Terri a temperament evaluation, a series of tests to evaluate any potential general aggressiveness in her. As I suspected, Terri passed with flying colors.

In addition, while working with the defense attorneys, I suggested they interview children in the neighborhood and depose the parents in the neighborhood to determine if Terri had ever shown any previous aggressiveness. Success again.

Also, depositions from the UPS driver, the mailman, and the paperboy all delivered just what I had suspected. The dog was gentle and friendly.

The case never went to court. It is usually quicker and cheaper for everyone to settle without a trial. Because I demonstrated in deposition that Terri was an otherwise well-behaved and gentle and friendly dog, it helped reduce excessive potential financial liability. And because the Browns had no prior knowledge of any aggressiveness from Terri, they had not been irresponsible by allowing children access to Terri and her puppies. Terri was a sweetheart.

I don't know if Mrs. Buford ever spoke to Mrs. Brown again. I sure hope so. Mrs. Buford, as much as anyone, realized how difficult it was to see your child hurt or threatened. Terri had felt the same way.

DOG BITES

Every dog is a potential biter. If your dog has bitten once and he bites again, your liability increases dramatically.

Part Two
Anxiety

*"You enter into a certain amount of madness
when you marry a person with pets."*
—Nora Ephron

*"Don't accept your dog's admiration as conclusive
evidence that you are wonderful."*
— Ann Landers

—————— **Chapter 10** ——————

JAY WALKING

In many ways Apache was a pretty typical Irish setter. Big, red, loveable, and a few points shy of life membership in Mensa.

Apache was a dog with two overriding passions: birds and a small dumbbell with feathers, his favorite toy. Apache spent the better part of his day pointing through the sliding glass door, or pointing and flushing his feathered friends in the backyard (where the Tubermans had installed a birdbath and two birdhouses), or mouthing his dumbbell. Apache never caught a bird, but the fun was in the pursuit, and each morning he would bound out the door in quest of the impossible dream.

The Tubermans did not have a particular problem with his bird chasing. True, the birds were being harassed, but no harm was done, and the birds still managed to negotiate getting their food and bath. Apache was resolute but not effective in his bird hunting.

Then came a rather unusual change, which prompted a request for my advice. Apache suddenly lost all interest in the great outdoors. Instead of springing out of the house each morning, he began slithering along the side of the porch, constantly looking up, then sneaking back inside the house. In fact, things got even worse. The Tubermans had trouble getting Apache outside at all, finally having to take him on the lead in the front of the house. Apache ventured into the backyard at night, but he remained uneasy. Inside the house, Apache still did a fair amount of pointing, even though his interest had waned. He was going through the motions, but his heart wasn't in it.

The Tubermans were perplexed. Was he sick? That was a fair question. Most of my cases are referred from the family veterinarian, who identifies purely medical issues, which may or may not impact behavior. Nevertheless, I still always ask a few basic questions to get a bigger picture of the animal's history.

"How is Apache's appetite?"

"Fine, Dr. Sampson."

"Any problems with elimination?"

"He seems fine to us in every way. Just that little skin problem...."

"Well, that would probably not have anything to do with...."

"...on top of his head."

"What do you mean, on top of his head?"

"Well, the rash is just on top of his head. Looks like little pimples."

I'm not sure if the light bulb went off on top of my head or the Tubermans' first, but it was clear that "top of the head" was the operative phrase here.

"You don't think, Dr. Sampson, that...."

"Yes, that's exactly what I think."

Poor Apache. It was starting to look like he had a role in the remake of Alfred Hitchcock's *The Birds*.

For the next several days, I had the Tubermans watch

their backyard through the living room window. Apache was still very hesitant about venturing out there, so it was impossible to confirm anything, but there was one piece of overwhelming circumstantial evidence: A large blue jay seemed to be pretty much in control of the backyard bird sanctum. He chased away other birds and even terrorized the squirrels. It was pretty clear that we had our culprit. At least we had a heads-up on the problem.

The issue here was to create an environment where bird and dog could live together. The blue jay was threatened by Apache, and Apache was now afraid of the blue jay. This was not the beginning of a lasting friendship. I had the Tubermans move the birdfeeder and bath to the side of the house and outside the fence so that Apache could still see the birds but could go outside without threatening his nemesis.

We slowly desensitized Apache to the outside area. I had the Tubermans begin by walking him through the yard during the darker hours, in the early evening or early morning. Each day they exposed him to more and more daylight. His walks were always accompanied by treats and obedience commands. As we have discussed, these commands embolden the dog by giving him a sense of what is expected of him and thus a feeling of security.

The backyard was becoming a safer place. Apache was now fed out in the back, given his beloved dumbbell, and praised for all his outdoor activities. The blue jay was happy, also. His gripe with Apache was never personal; it was all about territory, and both bird and dog were happy with the new arrangement.

A final note: Within weeks, Apache was completely at home in the backyard, pointing but not flushing the birds. But according to the Tubermans, he still shot an occasional glance toward the skies as he played outside. And, in case you still have any question about this case, the skin condition on his head cleared up as well.

DOG BITES

- A good anxiety reliever for your dog is to have him obey one of your commands. If your dog knows what to do in a stressful situation, he will be less stressed.

- When a dog's fear is exhibited, distract him by refocusing his attention on a favorite toy or treat.

- If your dog is slowly exposed to something that frightens him and rewarded with treats along the way, this will help him overcome his fear.

- You can get to a dog's brain through his stomach. This works for husbands, too.

———— **Chapter 11** ————

THUNDER DOG

Neighbors in the tiny rural town outside of Indianapolis were a bit curious when they noticed sisters Beatrice and Sybil, two middle-aged widows who lived together, out in their backyard shooting cap guns in the middle of the day. Local residents had always thought they were a bit eccentric, but this seemed particularly odd.

Well, you can blame that on me. It was my idea as part of a desensitizing program to help their Lab-shepherd mix, Heidi, get over her fear—her dread—of thunder, fireworks, and other loud noises.

This is a relatively common problem. Unlike humans, who are often afraid as children, some dogs do fine with loud noises until they age. Then their hearing wanes, and the distortion in the sound becomes unsettling. Other dogs are just born skittish and any loud or unfamiliar sound has the potential to be threatening.

Poor Heidi didn't know what to do with herself when she heard thunder. "Where's Heidi?" Beatrice and Sybil would ask during a storm. And like searching for Waldo, finding Heidi was quite a task. Was she behind the couch? Under the desk? In the basement? Behind the curtains? When she ended up under the covers in Beatrice's bed, I got the call.

It was clear from that first phone call that Beatrice and Sybil had already made the classic, but understandable mistake: They had been soothing Heidi when she panicked. They held her, they caressed her, they virtually slobbered all over her. And, as I mention elsewhere in this book, this gives the dog the idea that her agitation is being rewarded.

Rather than give you all the specifics of this case, I have listed here a few general guidelines for dealing with the fear-response to thunder. Every dog is different. It turns out that Heidi had a favorite ball, a spiny rubber sphere the sisters gave to her, that provided some solace during storms when she was stressed. It was her blankie, if you will. Heidi loved to retrieve it or just carry it around.

In fact, this approach worked so well that I took a call one night from the two sisters. "Dr. Sampson, I think you helped Heidi too much. We had a thunderstorm last night and she woke us up with that darn spiney ball at three in the morning to play."

So why were the sisters shooting cap guns in the backyard? If you read my list below, you will understand. I will tell you this: Heidi is no longer afraid of thunder/fireworks, but there are still a few neighbors petrified of Beatrice and Sybil.

TEN RULES FOR THUNDER/FIREWORKS

1. Don't reward your dog for his fear reaction. One method is to ignore him so he'll be comfortable when he is alone.

2. Let him seek his own place in the house. Since the noise will not hurt him, he will eventually associate his "spot" with safety.

3. Some dogs are sensitive to electricity in the air during storms. Rub them with an antistatic dryer sheet. That will "de-charge" the dog so he will not feel the electricity in the air during a strong electrical storm. Do not rub him as you would if you were petting him. The application of the antistatic material is not to be construed as a reward.

4. During the noise, if your dog pesters you for attention, don't soothe. One method is to give obedience commands to your dog. It will make him feel that when he "obeys" you, he will be safe. Knowing what to do relieves stress and builds confidence in the dog. But be sure to also rehearse obedience commands when storms/fireworks are not present so this is not foreign to him.

5. Distract the dog during the storm/fireworks with a positive experience like a favorite ball or special kind of playtime. In the case of Heidi, it was the spiny ball.

6. Desensitize the dog to storms by playing a tape of a storm. Throw in a few strobe lights. Be like a movie director. Create the scene and slowly increase the magnitude of the "storm." You slowly will be desensitizing your pet's fear. You can also, as numbers four and five suggest, associate that taped sound with positive experiences of obedience commands and play.

7. Continue to desensitize by shooting a cap gun or starter pistol in a box (so it is muffled) at a distance from your dog. Then slowly increase the intensity by moving closer and removing the gun from the box. Associate the scary sounds with something positive, as in numbers four and five. We want the dog to know that the noise poses no

threat. This must be done slowly. Do not reward the dog for responding in fear. If he shakes or seems nervous, cut back on the sound by increasing the distance.

8. Do *not* punish the dog for being afraid. That will make it worse. You will increase the dog's stress.

9. When you are gone from the house, be sure his "spot" is available as well as any toy or object that makes him feel safe.

10. During a storm, do *not* hide under the covers yourself. This sets a bad example.

DOG BITES

• If your dog has a special affection for a certain toy, it can be used as an effective motivator when shaping behavior.

• A dog that fears thunderstorms has a built in barometer. He'll know a storm is coming before you do. Unless you watch the Weather Channel.

——————— **Chapter 12** ———————

TALE OF A TAIL

After fifty-five years of marriage, the Goodbottoms had helped raise four kids, nine grandchildren, five great-grandchildren, and eighteen dogs (if you count the granddogs).

Their current dog was Maisie, a long-tailed terrier that must have seen a few too many cartoons on TV. Maisie spent much of the day chasing her tail. Round and round she went, but fortunately she never quite caught it. While the image is funny, the results of being successful at this endeavor can be serious. Dogs have been known to severely injure themselves in the pursuit or to have chewed and mutilate the tail once they make the conquest.

The Goodbottoms, unaware that this could be dangerous, thought it cute at first and did little to discourage it, although they became increasingly concerned that the increased frequency of occurrence was becoming compulsive and a problem. To make matters worse, the Goodbottoms had attempted to curtail the activity (excuse the pun) by distracting Maisie with a treat. Of course, this appeared to Maisie to be a reward for her persistence and only reinforced the behavior.

Then one day, by chance, Mr. Goodbottom was searching for something in the basement. The beam of his flashlight caught Maisie's attention, and she pounced on it like a cat after a mouse. Mr. Goodbottom chuckled and moved the light across the floor. Maisie bounded after it with the same passion and vigor with which she had pursued her tail.

Here was a classic case of good news/bad news. The good news was that inadvertently, the Goodbottoms had stumbled upon a method to refocus Maisie's behavior, redirecting her energy from tail chasing to the flashlight. But the bad news was that when the flashlight was turned off for more than a few minutes, Maisie went back to her tail. Then for some reason, Maisie's fixation with the flashlight translated into a fascination with shadows. Now Maisie had a triple addiction: her tail, the flashlight, and shadows.

The shadow obsession just seemed to grow worse. She jumped at doors, windows, any surface with any shadow or reflection. In the early morning, the Goodbottoms would hear a racket. It was Maisie leaping at the first rays of sunshine against the family room wall. It got so bad that the Goodbottoms had to keep the dog locked in their bedroom and sleep in total darkness to be sure that no shadow or reflection would arouse the dog. But apparently you can chase your tail in the dark. Nothing worked.

And when Maisie was outside in the fenced-in yard, the sun reflected off the metal roof of the shed, causing Maisie to constantly jump against the back door. Another racket that drove the Goodbottoms crazy.

When Mr. Goodbottom called, he was clearly sleep-deprived. First on the agenda was cutting off (not the tail—don't panic!) sources of light that created shadows. We placed black paper on the backdoor window and pulled curtains and blinds as the day progressed. We attached a six-foot nylon cord to Maisie so that when she did revert to any of these activities, she could be immediately shut down and tied to the leg of a chair or door knob. We did not want her to associate her compulsions with any attention of touch or voice.

More important, we wanted to refocus all this energy in ways that were more socially appropriate. I believe that in many cases like this, the dog is simply bored and will be happy with acceptable substitutes. The Goodbottoms offered a series of new toys, including Frisbees, rubber balls, and chew toys. Maisie was rewarded for learning to retrieve, which almost became an obsession. Maisie was like a kid at Christmas, throwing toys in the air, not sure which toy to play with first. Time spent playing with these toys was rewarded with a treat. And I also prescribed lots of walks and exercise, of course.

With the aid of a little antianxiety medication, Maisie soon got over her shadow stalking and tail chasing. But at night when Maisie curled up in her bed to sleep, she couldn't help stealing a glance at her tail. "So close," she must have thought, "and yet so far."

DOG BITES

- If you replace an unacceptable behavior in a dog, be sure you can live with the one you substituted.

- Tying a dog with a leash *in* the house is a good way to calm her and control unacceptable behavior.

- Medication is most beneficial when used in conjunction with proper behavior management.

- It is often difficult to squelch a dog's energy, but you can redirect it.

—————— **Chapter 13** ——————

HOME ALONE

Curly the cocker spaniel was enjoying his summer. What's not to enjoy? He spent the warm days with the Jacobson boys, who adored him. They all played ball; they even did a little swimming. Mom was always around to walk and feed Curly. They took car rides together. Curly stuck his head out the window and his ears flapped in the wind.

Yes, life was good. And then the summer ended.

Jake and Jordan went back to school. Mrs. Jacobson took a job teaching.

Poor Curly was just left in the house all day. No more ball playing, no more wind in the ears, no more swimming.

The end of the summer was…a bummer.

When the Jacobsons returned to their house at the end of the first day of school, they couldn't believe what they saw. Curly had had his way with the couch pillows, chewing one to bits and tearing up the others. There was evidence Curly had been scratching at the back door, and the neighbors reported that the cocker spaniel had been barking incessantly. Curly did not like being abandoned. At least, that's how he saw it.

No dog likes to be left alone, but the abrupt change

from the summer was Curly's fall, so to speak. The result was a classic case of separation anxiety, a disorder that can rear its ugly dread most often at times of year like this one, when the home situation changes.

The Jacobsons tried a few home remedies. Instead of letting Curly roam the house, they put him in the kitchen—a good idea if you are trying to reduce the amount of destruction, but a bad idea if you are trying to alleviate the dog's stress. In fact, the confinement many times exacerbates the problem. In this case, Curly became more anxious, chewed the kitchen table legs and the corners of the cabinets, and was found trembling and slobbering when the Jacobsons returned home.

Next, the Jacobsons confined Curly to a crate in the kitchen while they were gone. Crating a dog is a good idea, but not in response to separation anxiety, especially not so abruptly that it ends up making the problem even worse. Curly's confinement to the crate was the last straw. At the end of the day, the poor little pooch was a quivering mass of cocker spaniel, sitting in a puddle of his own saliva with bent cage wires all around him.

Home Alone might have been a great movie, but this was reality.

That's when I got the call—a call from people whose hearts clearly went out to Curly but who did not know what to do. They were aware they had actually made the problem worse.

The challenge was to make Curly comfortable in the crate. In theory, it is never too late to accustom a dog to a cage, but the earlier you start the better. Curly was four years old and had always enjoyed the run of the house, so this was a tough hurdle to overcome.

The first move was to have Curly sleep in the crate at night. A restful night of slumber would be a more pleasant experience than the fear and anxiety he felt when he was awake and isolated. To enhance that experience, I suggested that the crate be placed in the boys' room, close to his two favorite people—another attempt to connect the crate with a positive experience. Again, the message was simple: The crate is not a punishment, it's a cool place to hang out. A few treats for Curly when he was put inside were also suggested.

I asked that the boys take Curly out each morning and exercise him vigorously, hoping he would return to his crate and begin the day with a long nap, only to awaken a short time later to the sights and smells of the boys' room. This only worked partially. The dog was still anxious and didn't calm down much, but the boys fell asleep at school. Separation anxiety is not easily modified, and Curly still exhibited some signs of distress. When I again spoke to Mr. Jacobson…

"Well, it's the darnedest thing, Dr. Sampson. When Curly is in the house and I am outside, he goes bonkers, wanting to join me, unless I am mowing the lawn. Then he's fine."

My response was scientific.

"HUH?"

But apparently it was true. And after we did a little further testing we confirmed that even if Curly could not see Mr. J. outside the living room window all the time, the sound of the mower seemed to assuage his anxiety about being in the house alone.

My HUH soon turned into an AH HA! I told Mr. Jacobson to make an audio tape of the lawn mower sound.

"HUH?" he replied.

My initial analysis was obviously catching on. Yes, I told him, let's see what happens if we leave Curly alone in the crate with the sound of the lawn mower tape in the background for a short period of time.

We tried it. It worked. So we created a loop tape that would play all day and soothe Curly, who was happy that Mr. J. was in the yard working...and never questioned how fast the grass grew overnight. Or Mr. J.'s mowing during a snowstorm.

Ultimately, the tape broke, but the good news was that Curly had become so acclimated to the cage in the boys' room that he was comfortable spending the day there while the family was at school and work.

I loved this case. I remember laughing with Mr. Jacobson when he said, "When I mow, Curly is happy."

It's always fun when you get Mow and Curly in the same sentence.

DOG BITES

- A well-exercised dog is a good dog, especially when he is napping. Say good-night, Fido.

- Be sure your dog's crate is secure. One or two successful getaways and your dog will have a new recreational pastime: escaping.

- The best place for your dog's crate is in your bedroom. Both you and your dog will like being together. Unless one of you snores.

- If your dog barks when left alone in the car, give him a treat when you leave. By the time he eats it, you'll be out of sight. And out of mind.

—————— **Chapter 14** ——————

LITTLE MAC

Mr. McTavish, the fox terrier, had been through a lot. He spent the first few years of his life in a household with several children. On the surface, that sounds pretty good, but unfortunately, neither dogs nor babies come with instruction books on how they should be treated.

While abuse and neglect are sometimes difficult to legally identify, a dog knows it when he experiences it. Mr. McTavish (Mac) was basically shy and timid and now the victim of a vicious cycle. The children were not good caregivers, which made the dog skittish, unresponsive, and asocial. The result was that Mac spent much of the day hiding in his cage or behind furniture, avoiding interaction with the family. And the result of that was the family saw no reason to keep a dog that didn't want to be part of the group.

Mac was soon given up for adoption at a local animal shelter. Reputable shelters strive to be honest about their adoptions, thus avoiding placements that do not work, resulting in a dog that is either abandoned again or mistreated. The prospects for a happy home were not good for Mr. McTavish. The shelter could not have hidden his faults even if they had wanted to. Mac was visibly nervous and shy, and he stayed in the back of his cage when people observed him.

I am a big advocate of getting dogs from shelters, dog pounds, and humane societies, but I caution people to choose wisely and pick a dog that is a good fit with their circumstances. All canines come with a certain amount of emotional baggage, especially those that have spent a considerable amount of time with other families. Combine these experiences with dispositions that are inherent in certain dogs, and you realize you are adopting an animal that already has a very distinct personality. You may be able to shape his demeanor, but it won't happen overnight. So *please,* wait until the morning to call me.

The woman who adopted Mac did call me for help one day. Her heart had gone out to the dog when she first saw him at the shelter, and because Mrs. K. was part of a fox terrier rescue group, she felt even more motivated to help the little pooch.

Mrs. K. was not inexperienced in this area. She had rescued dogs before, but this was a challenge she had never faced. How do you begin to socialize a dog that spent most of the day shaking with its tail tucked between its legs and hiding in his crate? Mac was afraid of his own shadow, and it was a puny little shadow at that.

Mrs. K.'s initial handling of this problem was classically wrong, but understandably human. She reacted to the dog's fear response to noise, for example, by holding him and soothing him when he shook or cowered. Unless you just skipped to this chapter, you have probably already learned that this is a big no-no.

The dog was actually being reinforced by the soothing and praising of that behavior. He was being rewarded to stay hidden and away from people. Mrs. K. could always be counted on to come by with a few hugs and tummy rubs. Yes, he was starting to warm up to his owner. Why not? In a way, Mr. McTavish had actually conditioned Mrs. K. to come to him when he was nervous.

The only bright spot in this whole scenario was that Mac did seem to like other dogs. Mrs. K.'s daughter had a cocker spaniel, and the two seemed to hit it off when Dafney paid a visit. Mac was clearly a dog's dog, meaning that for whatever reason, he was far more comfortable with other dogs than with people. As you know, there are also people-people and dog-people. There are also people-dogs.

There are also dog-dogs. That's why some dogs love to go to Doggie Daycare.

It was now time to change Mac's view on life. Every moment that the dog remained alone (and unbothered) was further proof to Mac that his "I want to be alone" act had some value to him. I told Mrs. K. that when she returned from work, the dog was to be taken from the crate and that all bedroom doors were to be shut. There was to be no safe haven for Mac where he could avoid the world.

Mac was to be on a lead and encouraged (but not dragged) around the house and given treats as Mrs. K. tidied up, prepared dinner, or even watched TV. Mac needed to know that the house was a happy place and nothing would harm him if he wasn't hiding.

This also applied to the outdoors. Mrs. K. would go into the yard with Mac on a leash accompanied by treats for his entry into the real world. He was now being rewarded *not* for asocial behavior, but for his willingness to be genial—to be the kind of dog most people want. The treats came not when he was hiding under the bed, but were plentiful when he was comfortable in the yard with people or out for a walk meeting strangers.

Progress was understandably slow, but then I learned that Mrs. K. had a small business in her basement, an office that had a separate entrance. I only learned this after several phone calls, and Mrs. K. was perplexed that I thought it was an important piece of the puzzle. "Sometimes a solution is right under your nose," I told her. "Here it is right under your feet."

Mac now had a new gig. He accompanied Mrs. K. to work instead of spending the day in the crate. He started wondering what he had been hiding from his whole life. Within weeks, Mac was the official greeter to all of Mrs. K.'s clients. A tiny sign at the door to the basement office read: TAKE ONE/GIVE IT TO MAC. It was a box of dog biscuits.

Yes, life was good for Mac. True, he had to work nine to five, and the pay was lousy. But he had a great benefits package.

DOG BITES

- Spray the objects you don't want chewed with bitter apple. Then give your dog a healthy dose of bitter apple on its lips and mouth. Most dogs don't need a second reminder.

- If your dog could read, would you give it the same book every day? Try a variety of toys to keep it interested.

- Using a soothing, soft voice with an animal showing fear only reinforces the fear. Your best bet: Give him a command. He'll feel better knowing you are in charge when he needs to know what to do.

- Don't let a fearful dog hide in one place in the house. He needs to know that he can be safe throughout the house, not just under your bed.

————— Chapter 15 —————

FRAIDY DOG

Many calls I get come from new pet owners—people who are trying to cope with a problem they experience when bringing the dog or cat into the house for the first time and who want to nip that problem in the bud. Too many owners live with a problem for a long time, letting it fester. Bad idea.

But I also get many calls from long-time owners when problems surface as their pets age. As with people, the aging process can change behavior. An older cat or dog may have hearing loss, arthritis, or failing vision, which can cause compromised maneuverability. These can be accompanied by a related behavioral component. The animal makes adjustments either consciously or instinctively to cope with its changing body. Sounds familiar, doesn't it?

Lena was an eight-year-old Lab—not quite geriatric, but in the twilight of her retrieving career. Lena was a one-woman dog. She never let Mrs. Hogarth out of her sight. If she was walking and stopped abruptly, Lena would bump into her. It was amazing she didn't have a flat nose.

And the dog also required a great deal of attention. If

she wasn't constantly patted, praised, and rewarded, she would whimper, paw her, dig at the rug, and make a fuss to get more attention. She was becoming very insecure in her old age. Mrs. Hogarth compared Lena to her husband. "Edgar is also very high maintenance," she told me, "just like this dog."

Mrs. Hogarth, like many pet owners, didn't really have a problem with the dog's neediness. Truth is, most pet owners kinda dig that, although it has its drawbacks. Total dependence can lead to separation anxiety and, in some cases, discomfort with strangers. We want our dogs to love us, not worship us.

The problem was compounded because Lena was noise-sensitive. Virtually any noise out of the ordinary— and in some cases even familiar sounds—set Lena off. She would cower, pace, tremble, pant, shake, and dig at the rug. If she had been a toy poodle, she would have been a basket case.

Mrs. Hogarth even put up with that. Then one day I received a call from the shaken owner (there was a lot of shakin' goin' on in that house). A new stove had been installed in the kitchen, and when Mrs. H. turned it on there was an audible click—a click that threw the dog into a tizzy. This had apparently gone on for weeks. Mrs. Hogarth at first thought the dog was sensing a gas leak and was warning her. This made a great story at Tuesday night women's bowling league, but it wasn't true. The gas company made a few trips out to the house and told Mrs. Hogarth in no uncertain terms that while they respected the pooch's nose, their equipment detected nothing unusual.

Then there was the TV. Certain commercials set the

dog off. Every time she heard the Empire Rug jingle, for example, she had another panic attack. Interestingly, some commercials she liked, or at least ignored. Others she reacted negatively to. This is the kind of dog you need in a focus group.

She would run to the telephone and knock it off the base so it would stop ringing. Smart dog, but cell phones would have been trouble if she had lived to see one.

When Mrs. Hogarth called, I tried to zero in on her reaction to the dog when she responded to these sounds. It was clear that Mrs. Hogarth had compassion for the dog's situation. She would hold her, snuggle with her, lavish her with attention. Hey, why not? The dog was scared stiff.

I'll tell you why not! If there is one theme in this book, this is it: If you reward a pet, even inadvertently, for appropriate *or inappropriate* behavior, she will repeat that behavior. I'm not a psychiatrist, but you can take that advice to the bank with your children, your spouse, your annoying neighbor, and your boss. That's human nature. And canine nature. And feline nature.

So here's how Lena's two problems meshed into one: Lena was getting older. Her hearing was beginning to wane, so sounds were distorted, unfamiliar. The change in the frequency frightened Lena, and her fear response was rewarded by Mrs. Hogarth, who embraced the dog the way you would a child who feared a noise, like thunder. But there is a difference. Children can be reasoned with, talked to, and made to understand. A dog only responds to one thing: *Was I rewarded for my behavior?* And, indeed, Lena was. Big time.

To confirm my theory, I asked Mrs. Hogarth if the dog

acted this way with her husband. "Come to think of it, she doesn't," said Mrs. Hogarth. "Of course, my husband doesn't care much for the dog. He ignores her. Could that have anything to do with it?"

I have a great deal of patience with clients, but there are times when a big DUH would probably be appropriate. Since Mr. Hogarth paid no attention to the dog, there was no value in Lena doing her Don Knotts performance. Most parents know not to reward a temper tantrum. Same difference. The result was that the dog was first being scared by new sounds, then responding inappropriately, and then being rewarded.

I made several suggestions, including the obvious one, which was for Mrs. Hogarth to stop reinforcing the unwanted behavior and either ignore Lena or put her under obedience control during these times. I also suspected it was not Empire Rug that Lena had a problem with, but something about the frequency of that commercial and other TV spots that irked the dog. I suggested Mrs. Hogarth have the vertical and horizontal control on the TV adjusted, which altered the frequency of the TV sound. It worked.

Over time, Lena got a grip on things, or at least it appeared that way. Then one day, I received another call from Mrs. Hogarth. Lena was doing better, but when she was vacuuming the house she discovered that when Lena had her panic attacks she had scratched all the threads out of a large area braid rug, which completely fell apart.

I told her to call Empire Rug.

DOG BITES

• Rehearse obedience commands daily.
You'll feel like the boss. Practice makes
perfect. And you'll have an obedient dog.

• Occasionally, ignore your dog when he
appears fearful and anxious. He will learn
that when he is self-reliant nothing bad
happens to him.

Chapter 16

PRIMROSE PATH

I get many calls from clients whose pets are aging and who seek some advice on how they can best adjust to their pets' changing needs. But sometimes it is the owners who have a change in their health. Here too, accommodations must be made.

When Mrs. Primrose called, she had been through quite an ordeal. Although she had been pretty healthy in her senior years, her recent hip replacement surgery had set her back. And it had a devastating effect on Lizzie, their active but also aging standard poodle. Mrs. P. had done most of the dog walking in the family; her husband Herb was not in good health, himself.

When Mrs. Primrose began suffering with hip problems, her frequent medical appointments meant Lizzie spent periods of time alone in the house, a situation that she seemed to tolerate fairly well. But when Mrs. P.'s surgery finally came, Lizzie felt abandoned. Mrs. Primrose was hospitalized for more than a week. When Mr. Primrose would return home at the end of the day from visiting his wife at the hospital, he barely had enough energy to tie Lizzie outside for ten minutes before he went to bed. The next day, it was back to see his wife at the hospital, again leaving Lizzie alone for several hours at a time.

Lizzie started to exhibit classic signs of separation anxiety. She became nervous and started chewing on the back doorknob and began destroying the sofa pillows. Lizzie was bored, under-exercised, and stressed from being left alone. Despite her advancing age, Lizzie had a good deal of moxie left in her, and it was coming out in all the wrong ways.

When Mrs. Primrose returned home from the hospital, things still looked dim for Lizzie. The Primroses left the house for several hours each day so that Mrs. P. could take part in exercise sessions at the therapy center, where she walked on a treadmill. Upon each return from therapy, they saw the results of Lizzie's separation anxiety: The house was a mess, the door jams were chewed, and the linoleum had been scratched up.

I can only imagine Mrs. Primrose's surprise when I suggested that Lizzie get on the treadmill, as well. Odd as this may sound to you, it was not an unprecedented suggestion. Dogs have been trained to exercise on treadmills. And, in many cases, they love it. That was the case with Lizzie. Of course, it took a little getting used to, but the staff at the therapy center was helpful, and after a little encouragement and a learning period, Lizzie became an exercising fool. Soon Lizzie and Mrs. P. were side by side, having the time of their lives, but going nowhere.

In fact, Lizzie looked forward each day to her trip to the therapy center. So much so that when the Primroses were through with their sessions, they invested in their own treadmill so that both Mrs. Primrose and Lizzie could take turns enjoying the benefits of a brisk walk several times a day in the comfort of their home. Lizzie would sit and watch Mrs. P. walk on the treadmill; then Mrs. P. would take a break to read her newspaper and Lizzie would jump aboard.

Because Lizzie's separation anxiety continued to escalate when the Primroses were not at home, there was more to do. Lizzie needed to be re-introduced to her crate, which had not been used since housebreaking. This would be a place where she could stay when the Primroses were not home, but a place where she would feel secure and have no opportunity to displace her anxiety inappropriately. I suggested that the crate be moved to the master bedroom, where she would sleep in it every night with her owners right in the room, thus logging many comfy hours, reestablishing her affinity for the crate. The bedroom is usually the best place for a crate—a familiar place with familiar human odors.

Following a few weeks of her sleeping in her crate at night, the Primroses were to take many short trips away from the house, keeping Lizzie in the crate while a radio played in the background. The trips varied in length but were always short—about one to five minutes. When the Primroses returned, the radio was turned off. This reinforced to Lizzie that the music meant the Primroses would be home soon. Over a period of many weeks, they extended the length of their trips to as much as an hour (with shorter leaves of just a few minutes interspersed) and coupled them with exercise before leaving. The more Lizzie slept when they were gone, the less stress she would feel.

Mrs. Primrose recovered nicely from her hip surgery, but both she and the dog continued to walk the treadmill every day. Lizzie felt increasingly more comfortable about being left alone, in part because she was so exhausted from her exercise routine that she pretty much slept the entire time the Primroses were gone. A sleeping dog is a good dog.

Yes, Lizzie loved that treadmill, but you should have seen the expression on her face when Mr. Primrose bought his wife a stationary bike for Christmas.

DOG BITES

• When you leave your dog alone in his crate, reduce stimulation by turning down lights and closing blinds. The more he sleeps, the less anxiety he'll have.

• A crate is not a temporary solution to a problem. Your dog will look at it as his den if he is properly conditioned to it.

• Exercise is a good stress reliever. It stimulates body chemistry that induces calm.

———— **Chapter 17** ————

A NEW LEASH ON LIFE

Nobody was ever unhappier with the health care delivery system than Lucky. And that includes people in HMOs.

Lucky was a stray mutt. His vagabond life had been fraught with danger, and like so many other dogs with wanderlust, he found himself the victim of a hit-and-run driver whose SUV missed most of Lucky except for his left rear leg.

Lucky for Lucky (which wasn't his name yet), who should drive by but Sophie Schwartz, the quintessential little old lady, who found the ailing pooch on the side of the road and brought him immediately to the veterinarian for emergency care.

Lucky spent several days at the clinic, and while there is absolutely no reason to question the quality of the care he received, there is also little doubt that his stay was something less than pleasant. Almost a week of treatment for a crushed leg and hip is not a walk in the park—something Lucky was a long way from enjoying.

When Mrs. Schwartz finally took the dog home, she had already fallen in love with the little guy. (Wait a second, he wasn't little at all. He was seventy-five pounds, and all muscle.) Mrs. Schwartz, who had originally planned on putting the dog up for adoption, decided to keep Lucky.

Lucky was unfriendly—not aggressive, really, but certainly no social butterfly. But he loved Mrs. Schwartz's backyard, a safe haven for the former stray and a far cry from his previous life, where he spent most of his time just trying to survive. Yeah, the backyard was very comforting. "Why would I ever want to leave it?" thought Lucky.

During the months that followed, Lucky returned to the veterinarian several times—usually for a bit of rehab, but also for a pesky ear infection and, of course, for his regular check-ups.

And then, like a bolt of lightning, it dawned on Lucky. "The only time I ever leave this great backyard is to go to the doctor. I get to the clinic and he slides a thermometer up my rear, pokes at my leg, sticks some contraption in my ear, gives me injections, and squeezes my anal glands."

You couldn't put anything over on Lucky.

Of course, many dogs have some anxiety reaction when they pull up to the veterinary clinic. Our own hearts beat a bit faster when we see our dentist. But generally dogs have a more positive association with cars. They know they can stick their heads out the window; they know that the car may be headed for their favorite park or the drive-thru at the bank where a dog treat is always available.

Lucky had none of those experiences. Everything about that car meant trouble. Because every time Lucky got in the car, his luck just seemed to run out.

And because Lucky never went anywhere in the car except to the animal clinic, Lucky also knew that when Mrs. Schwartz put the collar around his neck, that meant a leash was coming. And that meant getting in the car.

And if you're reading this and don't know what getting in the car meant, then Lucky is smarter than you.

Every trip to the clinic became more traumatic. The dog was virtually uncontrollable in the car. He bordered on dangerous at the clinic and had to be muzzled.

That's when I got the call.

It was clear to me—and to Mrs. Schwartz—how this problem had perpetuated itself. Now we had to solve it.

I told Mrs. Schwartz that the dog needed to wear his collar twenty-four/seven. He needed to first learn that the leather around his neck was *not* a signal that he was going for a ride. Even that step required a good deal of work by Mrs. Schwartz, who had reached the point where she feared even showing Lucky the collar. I think Mrs. Schwartz felt like the mouse that suggested putting a bell around the cat's neck. It was a good idea, but who was going to do it?

Mission accomplished.

So, Lucky had his collar. He didn't like it, but happily he discovered that the leash never came, which meant he wasn't getting in the car, which meant... (Now you're catching on!)

Lucky paraded around the yard with his collar on. After several days, Mrs. Schwartz attached a six-foot cord to his collar and let it drag on the ground. Again, Lucky was anxious, but he soon realized he was not going to be yanked from the security of his backyard. For days he simply pulled his cord along the ground. Lucky was happy. He realized the leash did not mean going to the veterinarian.

That was fine, except that's exactly where we needed him to go.

At that point, I suggested to Mrs. Schwartz that we put on a head halter/collar, an incredibly effective and humane way of controlling a large animal, on Lucky.

If you can control his head, you can almost steer an animal as you would use handlebars to steer the front wheel of a bike. Where the head goes, the body will follow. That's why a child can control a horse that weighs several hundred pounds. "Would a gentle leader work on my husband?" asked Mrs. Schwartz.

We slowly conditioned Lucky to tolerate the head halter by associating its placement with treats and petting. Since there had been no previous negative experience with the head halter/collar, that part went relatively quickly.

Now it was time for a full desensitization program, a continuation of what we were doing, with an emphasis on getting Lucky in the car. But it had to be done slowly, a tiny step at a time.

Mrs. Schwartz took Lucky to the car, walked him around the car, let him look at the car. She opened the car door. She got in the car. She got out of the car. She gave Lucky a treat.

After a few days, Lucky got in the car and was rewarded with treats. Mrs. Schwartz started the engine, but she didn't go anywhere. More treats. Then she started driving around the block, returning Lucky to the backyard ten minutes later. More treats. Then the trips got a bit longer. Guess what? More treats. The trips got longer and included new areas.

The neighbors were beginning to talk.

Now it was time to drive to the clinic. Mrs. Schwartz had to feel she was pulling a fast one on Lucky, but there

Lucky got out and looked a little anxious. "I've been double-crossed," Lucky must have thought. He was shaken. But then Mrs. Schwartz took him home instead of entering the animal hospital.

Now that Lucky was desensitized to the car, he needed to go to the clinic several times. First they allowed Lucky to stay in the car; but the next time they brought Lucky inside. Then Lucky met the technician, who gave him treats.

Gee, this is taking forever, isn't it?

Indeed it did. Scores and scores of trips to the animal clinic, each leading to the inevitable face-to-face with the veterinarian.

Yes, finally Lucky was unafraid of going to the animal clinic. All was well. The vet was happy. Mrs. Schwartz was happy. Even Lucky was happy...about everything except having his anal glands squeezed.

DOG BITES

- If you only take your dog in the car when he's going someplace unpleasant, like the veterinary clinic, he could become anxious in the car. Take him to the bank frequently for a biscuit.

- Aggressive behavior is often driven by stress, anxiety and fear. If your dog is snarly, see if you can find out why.

- If you're using treats to reinforce appropriate behavior, don't fatten your dog up. Use low-fat varieties or use tiny bits of his regular food. Keep total daily intake of food about the same.

Part Three

Housebreaking/ Elimination Problems

*"I wonder what goes through [a dog's] mind when
he sees us peeing in his water bowl."*
—Penny Ward Moser

—————— **Chapter 18** ——————

DEAR JOHN

Here's something to keep in mind: When toilet training a three-year-old boy and housebreaking a dog, you should have similar aims.

Actually, the dog and the child should have a similar aim, as well. The child should get it in the toilet and the dog should be able to hit the grass. You wouldn't think that would be very hard. But you never met Bert, (that's the dog, not the child), a sixty-pound Dalmation.

Here's the story. I hope you're in the mood for a little bathroom humor.

The Wilsons had moved into a new house. Well, not really new at all. It was a rustic Victorian that had a lot of charm and a bathroom from the Middle Ages. The commode had been rebuilt, and the result was a protuberance of pipes that were retrofitted to the existing plumbing. Not pretty, but functional. The toilet was actually on a carpeted platform that covered the pipes a step off the ground.

The Wilsons' son, Ian, was being toilet trained. Like most little boys in the throes of toddlerhood, he needed a little direction. The step up to the high toilet didn't help. When Mr. Wilson came downstairs to use the bathroom, he surmised Ian needed more target practice. The bathroom was soaked, as though the little boy had been trying to put out a ground fire.

Mr. Wilson even tried to catch Ian in the act to see just what the problem was, but when he did manage to sneak up and peek in the door, he usually witnessed a bull's-eye performance. Watching Ian peein' wasn't solving the mystery, but it was a hoot to say out loud.

Mrs. Wilson, by the way, was nine months pregnant. She was in no position to, nor could she get in the position to, clean up Ian's messes. That's what dads are for.

One night while the family was watching TV, Mr. and Mrs. Wilson watched as their son got up and went into the bathroom. "Isn't that cute," said Mrs. Wilson, "how the dog always follows Ian into the bathroom?"

It was as if someone had hit Mr. Wilson over the head with a ten-pound bag of Purina. Sure enough, Mr. Wilson took another peek through the bathroom door just in time to see Ian hit a three-point swish while Bert went scoreless, hitting only the rim on all shots.

To this day, I am not sure how this dual approach began. Clearly Bert was motivated in part by the odors in the bathroom which were initially created before Ian became more adept at hitting the bowl. The dog loved Ian and followed him around most of the day, so naturally he walked into the bathroom with him and simply emulated his master. Now that we had determined what was happening, the question was how to break Bert's habits.

Keep in mind that Bert still was going outside, but male dogs are notorious for storing urine (usually for the purposes of marking their territory) and then pumping it out on demand. Bert was a classic case. When the

Wilsons returned home at the end of each workday, Bert, who had been crated eight hours, ran outside and made a token urinary gesture, then bounded back in the house to see the family and get a treat. No matter. He knew he could go later with Ian.

The problem we faced was more logistical than psychological. The dog was basically housetrained; he was just engaging in a few extracurricular activities. My first suggestion was a door closer—a spring-loaded hinge that would slam the door shut before Bert had a chance to follow Ian into the john. Then, to further reward Bert's appropriate behavior, I encouraged the Wilsons to walk outside with the dog when they came home so he would urinate multiple times. Each discharge resulted in a treat, reducing his desire to make a bee-line back to the house. Bert got a treat for "going," not for going back to the house. We did not want to pay him for coming in the front door.

In addition, Bert was confined to the crate at night to prevent a midnight trip somewhere else in the house.

I doubt that Bert was really copying the youngster's behavior, but wouldn't you love to have seen the smirk on Ian's face every time he used the bathroom while Bert did his thing in tandem. I'm just glad we figured this out while Ian was a toddler. This is not the kind of ammunition you want to give a teenager.

DOG BITES

- Accompany your dog outside to eliminate when you arrive home. If you wait at the door, he may head back to the house without finishing his business. Hey, he's missed you!

- If your dog has an elimination problem, control his intake of water (as you would food) to reduce excessive drinking.

- Dogs hold urine for marking and seldom empty their bladders completely. Everybody's gotta go, but dogs gotta go and go and go again. Give them time.

- Reward elimination immediately when it occurs. Don't wait at the door with a treat. Wait at the dog with a treat.

—————— Chapter 19 ——————

WHIZ KID

I want to give you, the reader, a leg up on something: getting a leg up.

This is the story of Buddy, a perfectly respectable male Boston terrier that, like everyone from Boston, had impeccable manners and meticulous bathroom habits. So the Guggenheims were surprised when they began to find evidence of Buddy's apparent regression in bathroom decorum. The leg of the couch had traces of urine, and the door jamb and the table legs were also slightly moistened. There were tiny drops everywhere.

Because the amount of urine was small and on vertical services, like a table leg, it indicated the dog had not squatted but had obviously lifted his leg. The Guggenheims assumed that Buddy was not really urinating out of need, but simply marking his territory. This is a very common and logical assumption to make, especially in a neutered male dog. But it is often wrong.

First of all, there is little reason for a single dog to mark his territory inside his home. There is no dog competition, so there is no need to claim his territory. The dog already sees the home as a secure place to eat and sleep, and not a place (when he is properly housebroken) to go to the bathroom.

At first, the Guggenheims ignored the problem. There were only traces of urine, but more important, there was no way to reprimand the dog because Buddy always avoided the limelight. He would urinate when the Guggenheims were asleep or in the other room watching TV. As you all know, punishing a dog after he has broken housebreaking guidelines is at best worthless and at worst confusing to the dog (and such confusion could create other problems). The Guggenheims didn't know where to turn. But wherever they turned, there was always a little bit of urine.

At some point, Buddy probably had an accident in the house when the Guggenheims delayed an outing due to bad weather or missed a scheduled walk. "Wow, that was sure easier than going outside," he may have thought (assuming dogs have thoughts).

Since there was no consequence to this previously forbidden behavior, Buddy did it again. And again. And so began a vicious cycle. And because Buddy suffered from a touch of separation anxiety anyway, the idea of staying closer to the Guggenheims made the new arrangement even better. Why go outside in the backyard, alone, when you can stay near Mr. and Mrs. G.? He turned into a sneak.

Now Buddy could eat in one part of the house, sleep in another, and urinate in a third area. What a floor plan! Of course, Buddy still urinated outside if he was walked by the Guggenheims, but now the formal living room was his own porta-potty as well.

First and foremost, the Guggenheims needed to know that Buddy was probably *not* marking his territory. He was urinating, pure and simple. And the faster they recognized that, the better understanding they would have of my suggestions. Teaching a dog to do something counter to his evolution (like *not* marking territory) is much harder than nudging him to follow his basic inclination (not to urinate inside where he eats and sleeps).

The Guggenheims were initially surprised when I told them they were not walking the dog enough. Many dog owners think that two or three times a day is plenty. I asked Mr. and Mrs. G. how many times a day they answered nature's call. I don't usually pose such personal questions, but I made my point.

I learned that the Guggenheims had been rewarding Buddy with a biscuit for his return to the house after being let out. As I have said before, this is a recipe for trouble. Dogs instinctively hold urine as a means of communication with other dogs. So when Buddy passes a fire hydrant, he can say in his own way, "My name is Buddy, I'm a Boston terrier, and I was here." Of course, a previous message may also have been left: "Hello, I'm Max the basset hound, and I was here first."

So when a dog goes outside, he has two motivations not to empty his bladder. One, he wants to get back inside for a treat, and two, he may want to communicate again real soon. Kinda like call waiting.

I told Mr. and Mrs. G. to always accompany Buddy outside, then reward him with a treat immediately for the act of urinating or defecating—and not for returning to the house for a treat. And I told them to make sure the dog goes several times, followed by a treat each time.

"I think he's shooting blanks," said Mrs. G. one day on

the phone, "just so he gets a treat." Buddy was no dummy. He realized his urine had value, and he often lifted his legs fifteen times on walk, which meant fifteen biscuits.

I'm glad she couldn't see my big grin.

"Now, reward him intermittently, like every other time, or every third time. As long as he thinks he may get a treat, the reinforcement will be effective," I told her.

I encouraged them to keep Buddy in their bedroom at night with the door closed, knowing that the canine instinct is to refrain from soiling where he sleeps.

And if the Guggenheims were watching TV and not monitoring him, I told them to keep Buddy on a leash tied to their chair to avoid the possibility he would sneak off to eliminate in another room. They were breaking his habit.

In order for Buddy to tell them he wants to go out, I also recommended hand watering. Rather than keep an endless supply of water in a bowl, I suggested that the bowl be down and empty when the Guggenheims were home.

When the dog checked or pushed his bowl around, he was to be given a limited amount of water immediately and then taken outside, reinforcing the signal to go out. This sets up a new connection in Buddy's mind: I drink; therefore, I urinate. And then I get treats. I also cautioned them to keep the toilet seat down so he wouldn't drink from the bowl.

It took several weeks for all this to work. But finally there were no drops of urine on the door jambs, the couch leg, the bookshelf, or the umbrella stand.

The rain of terror was over.

DOG BITES

- If your adult dog urinates in the house, he's probably not marking his territory; he's just messing up your furniture. Back to house-breaking 101.

- Be sure to take your dog outside several times a day. Not sure how many? Keep a record of your own habits. That will give you a pretty good idea.

- You don't have to reward your dog with a treat every time he urinates. Think of yourself as a slot machine and your dog as a compulsive gambler.

- Do not offer opportunities for your dog to exhibit bad habits. If he likes to piddle in the corner of the den, put a chair there. Better yet, keep him out of the den.

- If the dog defecates in the house, try feeding it half as much twice a day. This will reduce the intensity of the need to go.

—————— **Chapter 20** ——————

DOUBLE DRIBBLE

Mr. and Mrs. Breitbart had a King Charles spaniel named, what else? Sir Charles. Pee Wee or Puddles might have been better suited. I think you know where I'm going with this.

Too bad Sir Charles didn't know where *he* was going.

When Mr. Breitbart arrived home from work, Sir Charles apparently got so excited that he piddled all over himself and on the floor. Mr. B. just assumed the dog was just so overwhelmed to see him that he couldn't control himself. At first Mr. Breitbart didn't mind. He had never gotten that kind of response from Mrs. Breitbart.

But it was a problem. And the cause of the piddling wasn't quite what Mr. B. thought. We frequently refer to it as: *canine-greeting with submissive urination, and driven by excitement.* Excuse the expression, but that's a mouthful.

Yes, some dogs will urinate a bit when they are happy to see their owner, but the cause goes a bit deeper and farther back in the dog's ancestral history. Wolves, when meeting a pack member of superior status, will often hunker down and urinate. This is a show of submission and it survives today in the domestic dog, especially in dogs who are by nature less dominant or, to use a human term, shy and timid.

When the problem worsened and I was asked to help, the most important piece of information I garnered was that the dog did *not* do this when *Mrs.* Breitbart came home. The reason was that Mrs. Breitbart did not "excite" him, seldom greeting him by name and fussing over him. Then I asked what they had done to address the problem.

The Breitbarts' response to this was pretty typical. Most people recognize that punishment is not in order here. It's pretty obvious that the dog is not "going in the house." But the initial reaction is to save the carpet. When Mr. Breitbart got home, he would usher the dog outside quickly before Sir Charles had a chance to eliminate, then pet and excite the dog, causing him to urinate.

This response may save the carpet, but it is counter-productive to solving the problem. Think of it from the dog's perspective: "My owner comes home; he takes me outside right away; I roll over on my back, excited; pee all over the place; he pets me and says GOOD BOY. Oh boy, let's do this again tomorrow. Tomorrow I may do it in the house."

The real issue is that Mr. Breitbart had to considerably reduce the dominance threat and excitement he posed to Sir Charles and reduce the level of excitement he caused. Because the husband was bigger and more foreboding than Mrs. Breitbart, Sir Charles was intimidated and excited by his owner's arrival. He wasn't really scared of Mr. Breitbart, but his natural instinct said, "Let's not take any chances, here. Let's do that submissive/happy thing."

Mrs. Breitbart had a role to play as well. It was

important that Sir Charles be walked or let out before Mr. B. arrived home. True, dogs do save urine for marking, but the less ammunition, the better and the easier to control.

Sir Charles needed to be on a lead when Mr. Breitbart got home to facilitate going outside and not having to touch him, which increased the excitement. We established an area where he was tied away from both the door and Mr. B., thus reducing the anxiety.

We had to de-emphasize the pageantry of Mr. Breitbart's arrival. He was no longer to come in the house and call and greet Sir Charles. Instead, he was to enter uneventfully and ignore Sir Charles, avoiding even initial eye contact.

Within about three to five minutes, Mr. Breitbart could slowly reestablish communication with Sir Charles, at first with only a peripheral glance. I also cautioned him to speak softly, bend down to the dog's level, and pretty much look as non-threatening as possible. Mr. B. was six-foot-six and had a deep voice. This wasn't going to be easy.

And in a salute to Pavlov, I had the Breitbarts further condition Sir Charles so that any ring of the doorbell meant a treat, a result easily managed by ringing the doorbell but harnessing Sir Charles to a lead away from—but still in sight of—the front door, a place where Sir Charles could ultimately expect a biscuit. Why? We wanted the doorbell to redirect his attention and mean good things, not the possibility of a threatening person, even a familiar one, entering the home and exciting him. Arriving guests would give treats after they had ignored Sir Charles and let him settle down for several minutes.

The Breitbarts were fast learners, which always

translates into a successful intervention. Mr. Breitbart remained a bit intimidating to Sir Charles, but Mr. B. was still treated to a wet kiss now and then. Considering the alternative, this was an improvement.

DOG BITES

- If your dog submissively/excitement urinates when you greet him, restrain your own enthusiasm and calmly offer a treat. This refocuses the dog's attention and prevents urination.

- Don't punish a dog's submissive/excitement urination. That will make things worse.

- Guests frequently stimulate submissive/ excitement urination in a dog. Have guests initially ignore the dog. Minutes later they may interact and offer a treat.

- Don't cause submissive/excitement urination outside. The problem will then persist inside.

———— **Chapter 21** ————

FINE FOR LITTERING

Cat owners often rejoice that, unlike a dog, their pets usually require no special training to learn how to deposit their waste in the proper place. It's just instinctive and reinforced by their mother. Housebreaking a dog, despite what every book says, can be troublesome at times. And it takes a little work on the part of both the pooch and the owner. For cat owners it's a slam dunk.

Usually!

Surprisingly, I have received dozens of calls over the years from frustrated cat owners who claim that their cat seems to have missed the boat when it came to acquiring this instinctive behavior. Or, in some cases, the cat has the instinct, but what he is missing is the box.

When Edgar and Twila Crookshanks called me one morning about their cat, Ching, I listened carefully as the elderly couple took turns on the phone expressing concern about their cat's apparent disregard for what should have been basic instinctual behavior: Deposit waste in the sand; cover it up; catch mice.

Instead, Ching was leaving his waste alongside the box. Unlike other cases I had dealt with where the feces was a long distance from the box, these deposits had just barely missed the receptacle. Same with the urine. Usually when cats avoid their litter box, they *really* avoid it, often opting for a corner in another room.

I went through my normal litany of questions about the cleanliness of the box, explaining that some cats are so fastidious that they will not eliminate in a box that is soiled at all. In fact, most cats want to urinate and defecate in different recptacles. I told the Crookshanks that the rule of thumb for boxes is to have at least two boxes for one cat and three or four boxes for two cats. And as cats age, they become even more meticulous about their boxes. Just like humans, when cats get older, they get a bit more finicky.

After following my advice, another call made it clear that none of this seemed to address the problem. When I was assured that the boxes were kept scrupulously clean, I suspected that the problem might be the litter itself. I recommended that they "slope" the kitty litter in the box (three inches on one end, sloped to one quarter-inch for the last third of the box) affording the cat firm ground on one end of the box to get his footing. Many cats are spooked by the shifting "sands" of kitty litter, which is why many cats prefer your carpeting with its solid base.

After these further changes it was obvious that this was not the problem, either. At that point, I suspected that their dog, Pepi, a French poodle, might be the source of the enigma. Dogs are attracted to kitty litter boxes because the feline waste is considered a delicacy by canine gourmets. It smells good, it tastes good, and you can eat it fresh out of the box.

As a result, some dogs will practically stalk the family cat, waiting for him to leave a treat behind. Cats, who already prefer privacy in these matters, may opt to find another option for their daily squat rather than contend with a dog whose motto is: Waste makes taste.

Again, my thoughts did not seem pertinent to this case. But after the third phone call, I sensed there was something that I wasn't being told or had failed to understand. I often get that feeling. Information is seldom withheld on purpose by a client; instead, data goes undisclosed because the client doesn't think the behavior in question is relevant. Of course, I could blame myself for not soliciting the necessary facts, but I'll let you decide.

During this phone call I was once again desperately seeking a clue to this mystery, when Mrs. Crookshank, who was on the extension phone, casually said to her hubby, "Edgar, did you ever tell Dr. Sampson about Pepi's weird behavior?"

"Oh, sweetheart, don't be silly. What could that possibly have to do with the problem?"

I was beginning to see some light at the end of the puzzle. Animal and human behavior in a family are often connected. If they had a dog that was doing something a bit odd, it could clearly have something to do with the cat's eccentric conduct.

"What is Pepi doing?" I asked, and held my breath. I could almost see it coming.

Mr. Crooskshank explained that ever since his knee surgery, he hadn't been able to walk Pepi as often, a change of events that altered the normal constitutional activities of his dog. To compensate, Pepi had begun using the litter boxes—an unusual but not unheard of situation.

The result, of course, was that no self-respecting cat would share a bathroom with a French poodle. Or a German shepherd. Or an Irish wolfhound. It didn't matter where you were from. This was a private bath.

The solution was simple. We jerryrigged the door of the "cat" room with a chain that kept the door ajar so only the cat could fit through, then provided Pepi with his own litter box. This made Pepi very happy. He was pretty sure he was the only French poodle in the neighborhood with his own private litter box.

The Crookshanks even put a little sign on his box: NO CATS ALLOWED!

DOG BITES

Kitty litter is for kittens/cats; puppy litter and pads are for puppies/small dogs. If you require an alternative to walking your dog, check out this option at your pet store.

Part Four

Destructive Behavior

"My husband and I are either going to buy a dog or have a child. We can't decide whether to ruin our carpets or ruin our lives."
—Rita Rudner

_____ **Chapter 22** _____

BEING A LITTLE CHEWSY

Mrs. Rimple lived with her companion, Misty. Misty had a thing for the TV remote, and this drove Mrs. Rimple crazy. Misty was obsessed with it, hardly paying any attention to Mrs. Rimple at night. It was all about that TV remote.

Misty was acting like a husband. But she was a rottweiler puppy. Actually, Mrs. Rimple's husband was very attentive. Why not? He never knew where the TV remote was.

Let me explain. Misty was a chewer—a heroic chewer. All dogs, especially younger ones, not only love to chew, they need to. Like babies, everything passes through their mouths. It helps them to teethe, it loosens the first set of choppers, and it's a good form of exercise. In some cases, it is a way to reduce boredom. Chewing is like eating. Dogs are gonna do it. In fact, they gotta do it. But you can direct both activities so they are socially and medically beneficial.

I have had many calls over the years from people surprised that their dogs seem to zero in on things like eyeglasses, hearing aids, shoes, and, well, TV remotes, BIG TIME. Not so strange, really, when you realize that objects like these smell like YOU. I guess we should find this flattering.

Of course, Misty was interested in more than just TV remotes. Nothing, absolutely nothing, was safe. Her conquests included piano legs, computer cords, throw rugs, pencils, pool cues, throw pillows, and newspapers. Misty even had her way with a door knob. That's determination.

Some chewing is stimulated by boredom, lack of exercise, and separation anxiety, but in this case, Misty just had an overactive mastication. If this happens with your pet, don't set the dog up to fail. In other words, there is no benefit in tempting him with forbidden objects and no value in removing those objects and punishing him. When removing the unacceptable toy, I told the Rimples, always substitute an acceptable toy. The message that some things you can chew and some things you can't is not easy to fully grasp.

In addition, letting an untrustworthy dog wander the house creates too much temptation. Restriction of freedom can be helpful. Tie the dog close to you, block of certain areas with baby gates, or confine your dog in a crate when you can't watch her.

When dogs have a choice, they will go for the tastier item. Most dogs would prefer a piece of rawhide soaked in beef bouillon to a cue stick, but all dogs are different and the key is to find what turns your pooch on. If the things he craves (like your eyeglasses) are off-limits, keep them away from him. If you can't, try the bitter apple approach (see Page 86).

While you do want to provide objects of desire, you do not want to create an obsession. It's okay if your dog loves his rawhide bone from the pet store, but if he growls at you when you take it away or when you come near him, that's a bad sign. Items like that should be taken away. For good. Don't set the dog up for failure.

On the other hand, when Misty was chewing on something acceptable—like a Nyla bone—I had Mrs. Rimple teach the drop command, remove the item for a moment, and give Misty a treat, then return the bone. Eating is still a notch above chewing to dogs. In this way, Misty was rewarded for chewing something acceptable and for responding properly to its removal.

Misty had been given too many chewing choices, which made clear distinctions even harder. Dog toys had been strewn around the house, giving the message that anything on the floor is okay. But it's not okay. Misty had been confused. In addition, there were too many items around that looked similar. Rawhide bones were okay, pencils were not. Again, this sets the dog up to fail.

When Misty was cut off from temptation and rewarded for appropriate choices, she fared quite well. This is a great way to raise a child. Why not try it on your dog?

DOG BITES

• When a dog is chewing something unacceptable, remove it, admonish him, and give him something you both are happy with. Someone tell that to Weight Watchers.

• When your dog is chewing something appropriate, praise him and give him a treat. He needs to know what is right—not just what is wrong.

• Rotate toys to avoid boredom.

• Dogs sometimes become protective of their toys, especially the rawhide variety. If you see this happening, remove the rawhide. For good. Oh, and be careful. Don't set the dog up to lose.

—————— **Chapter 23** ——————

GOLD DIGGERS

We've all heard the expression "Making a mountain out a molehill."

This story is about Tom and Jerry, two golden retrievers who made a mess out of a molehill.

Here's the dirt: The story begins with Tom, a four-year-old typical golden retriever who loved to play. And also dig. Most retrievers are *not* inveterate diggers—that's a trait usually reserved for other breeds like wire-haired terriers and schnauzers.

But apparently Tom had not read *The Big Book of Dogs*, because Tom loved to dig. And dig. And dig.

His quest was not unfocused; he was on a search-and-enjoy mission to find moles. And moles there were. Tom lived adjacent to a wooded area replete with various forms of wildlife, so the moles crept in through his Invisible Fence area. And Tom made sure they didn't creep out.

The Culbertsons had some mixed feelings about the digging. True, the lawn was being destroyed, but the pesky moles were being eliminated. Ultimately, the Culbertsons decided to get a new dog, and in the back of their minds I am sure they felt that this distraction might squash a little bit of the digging initiative.

The idea backfired.

The new golden puppy was aptly named Jerry. And Tom became a perfect mole model. The Culbertsons never knew what hit them.

Jerry was truly on a mission. As he grew and matured, his love of digging surpassed even Tom's. The yard now looked like a minefield. Jerry seemed content whether he found a mole or not. He just loved to dig. Man, did he love to dig. In fact, Jerry was so good at it that Tom just kind of laid back and watched the dirt fly. Mole digging for Tom had now become a spectator sport.

Then Jerry began to develop a strange habit that had the neighborhood freaked out. When Jerry did find a mole, he not only killed it, he chomped on it until it was as flat as a pancake. And then—oh, you'll love this—when neighbors walked by, Jerry waited until they crossed the invisible fence field to pet and talk to him, at which time he deposited a flattened mole at their feet. YUK!

So how do you stop a dog from digging? I mean, birds gotta fly, fish gotta swim. Dogs dig for several reasons. First, it is part of their hunting instinct, which is why some breeds are more adept at it than others. Some dogs often dig out of boredom or to relieve stress. Others are just looking for a cool place to lie down. Some may be trying to escape or to find their owners.

The key here was not to isolate the exact reason that Jerry was a canine backhoe, but to find a way to channel that energy into a more socially acceptable pastime. My initial suggestions included an exercise program so that he would be too bushed to burrow. I also encouraged the Culbertsons to rid the outside area of moles in a more traditional way (see *The Big Book of Gardening*).

Eliminating the temptation goes a long way in stopping unwanted behavior. If Jerry did dig, they were to quickly reprimand him and remove him from the site.

And finally, I asked the Culbertsons if they could designate a digging area in part of the yard where Jerry's natural instinct to excavate could be realized in a less destructive way. If you build it, he will dig, I told them. And so he did.

Jerry loved his little "playground." The Culbertsons had built a six-foot-square play box of sorts, filled with moist sand. Not only was it in a nice cool area of the backyard, but I encouraged the Culbertsons to frequently bury an assortment of doggie treasures. When Jerry started to dig, he was quickly rewarded with rawhide bones, treats, and toys that he found under the sand. Why dig anywhere else?

Tom and Jerry remained fast friends. Jerry still thought it was very cool to tunnel all day. And Tom thought it was really hip to just watch.

Ya dig?

DOG BITES

For recreation (both yours and the dog's) construct a sandbox and bury treats in it for his digging pleasure. Build it and he will play.

Part Five

Other
Misbehaviors

*"Any time you think you have influence, try ordering
around someone else's dog."*
—The Cockle Bur

"If your dog is fat, you aren't getting enough exercise."
—Unknown

————— **Chapter 24** —————

NO BARKING ALLOWED

Barkley's name said it all. And if you lived in the same house as Barkley, you heard it all. In fact, you could hear him all over the neighborhood. Barkley was a barker. The little sheltie barked when the furnace kicked on, when the phone rang, when he heard people outside, when Mrs. Gelbard loaded or unloaded the dishwasher, when the doorbell rang, when the wind whistled through the trees, when the garage door opened, when the garage door closed.

The Gelbards also had three kids. The kids couldn't be quiet either, but that was not my problem. I do pets. "Please help us, Dr. Sampson," said Mrs. Gelbard over the phone one morning. I think that's what she said. It was hard to tell with Barkley barking in the background.

Dogs that bark at outside noises are reinforced in two seemingly paradoxical ways. The dog barks as part of his job as a sentinel or lookout for the pack/family. The alphas (the family members) respond by coming into the room, answering the door, or looking out the window to see why he is barking. Mission accomplished. In other cases, the dog comes to realize that when he barks at the UPS truck or the mailman, they seem to go away. "Hey, I'm doing my job," he thinks. It's hard to argue with success.

To combat this inadvertent reinforcement, we first eliminated as many sources of outside stimulation as possible. I had the Gelbards move some furniture around to cut him off visually from the outside and use the blinds to keep Barkley from seeing kids and FedEx drivers. Outside in the yard, a shadow box fence allowed Barkley to see through the slats, so we added some additional boards to prevent him from peering into the street.

Barkley also needed some extracurricular activity and more exercise to tire him out and distract him from his number-one pastime. The Gelbards introduced some new toys, increased the play time with him outside, and walked him daily.

But all this alone would not have been enough. Barkley's bark was too easily aroused by any disturbance. He needed to learn the meaning of QUIET. And I shouldn't have capitalized that word because I really didn't want the Gelbards to scream it. This confuses the dog into thinking you are barking with him. He thinks it's okay for everyone to make a lot of noise. You must say the word firmly, but not loudly.

Here is also a case where saying "quiet" and accompanying the command with a squirt from a water bottle is sufficient negative feedback to begin eliminating the yapping. A spritz in the face is nothing to sneeze at. But apparently it *was* something to bark at. Now he was barking at the water bottle. The dog was relentless.

Time to up the ante. The next step up was a bitter apple spray, an unpleasant concoction (purchased from any pet store) that many dogs can tolerate in tiny doses, so it works best when the pet has been given a strong dose on his lips and mouth so that the very smell becomes a deterrent (care must be taken not to get it in the eyes). In this case, Barkley needed to be on a six-foot lead inside the house so that when he did bark, he could be caught and commanded to be quiet and given (or simply shown) the bitter apple. Threat of this kind of punishment can be just as effective as punishment itself.

Immediate correction is crucial. Barkley needed to know that if he barked, there was an immediate consequence. Without the lead, he would have quickly learned he could bark and then high-tail it out of the room. This was not a game. The Gelbards used the same approach when he was in the yard, reeling him in on an even longer cord when he barked and saying "quiet."

What about collars that spray citronella in the dog's face or give a shock, or collars or devices that emit high-pitched frequencies? They can be effective and I am not opposed to them in principal, but they are not my first choice. They can be appropriate, however, when the dog is left alone outside during the day or is alone in an apartment all day. Again, not the best first line of defense, but appropriate in some cases.

Within a couple of weeks, Barkley learned what the word "quiet" meant and was getting the message that his barking had some negative consequences. It was soon after that when I received a final call from the Gelbards.

"Barkley has made a dramatic improvement. He's a different dog. Dr. Sampson, I don't know how to thank you."

That time, I heard her loud and clear.

DOG BITES

- Don't shout your command if you want your dog to stop barking. He'll think you're barking along with him.

- Your dog is a sentinel. He barks at noises to alert you and summon you to his side for support. If you're not home, the dog might not be as vocal with an intruder. He knows there's no one to heed his call.

- Shock, citronella, and high-frequency collars can be effective, but if you choose to use one, follow the manufacturer's directions carefully. If you don't, the effect of the feedback may actually exacerbate the barking.

——————— **Chapter 25** ———————

STAR SEARCH

Here's the dilemma I was confronted with when I received a distressed phone call from a couple very much in love. They were having relationship problems. It wasn't that they were fighting like cats and dogs. It was their cats and dog that were fighting like cats and dogs.

Lois loved her cats. Jim loved his dog. Lois loved Jim. Jim loved Lois. There was no more love to go around.

Here were the culprits in this feud: two black cats named Sirius and Vega, a three-legged cat named Rigel, and a dog named Tippy. Tippy was a Scottie, a breed of dog that traditionally has little tolerance for rodents or cats. I'd be tempted to say that many Scotties are cat haters, but that would be unkind. It would not, however, be untrue.

Jim and Lois wanted to make a perfect blended family, but their approach was somewhat analogous to putting olive oil and water in a blender. Bursts of activity, a lot of noise, but a waste of time. When Jim brought Tippy to Lois's house, there was total chaos. The cats freaked out. One hid behind the dryer, one hid in the pantry, one jumped on top of the counter, one hid under the bed, one hid in the basement, and one hid under the couch.

Wait a second, that's too many cats. Well, it seemed like there were cats hiding everywhere.

If the cats were taken to Tippy's house, they panicked even more. Not familiar with the terrain, they didn't know where to hide. Tippy got very protective of his turf. It was like a search-and-destroy mission. Remember how cartoonists draw cats that are scared, with all four limbs extended in mid-air, hair standing straight up? That's it. You've got the picture.

Jim and Lois had already delayed their marriage for more than a year. I explained to them that this hostility between dog and cat was certainly not a new problem. True, many felines and canines live happily together, but there exists a predisposition to mistrust each other. This mistrust only goes back ten thousand years in history, so I figured I could wrap this baby up with a couple of phone calls. Yeah, right.

The first issue was where the newlyweds should live after the marriage. Believe it or not, this was an important decision to make regarding the animals. In either case, there was bound to be unrest, but I determined that the cats would be more comfortable in their own home. Dogs are instinctively guardians of their territory, so we didn't want to give Tippy home field advantage.

It's always difficult to tell clients that part of the problem lies with them. Actually, most of the problem lies with them, but I have to be a diplomat. In this case, Jim needed to exercise a bit more control over the dog. We began by placing Tippy on a lead. But even if his movements were restricted, his barking scared the bejeebers out of the feline triumvirate. To squelch the yapping, we used a squirt from a water gun in Tippy's face, preceded by the command "quiet." This doesn't hurt, of course, but it's a nice dose of reality and I think a touch humiliating, as well. He soon stopped barking when he heard the command and saw the water bottle. This was a big step toward the cats' peace of mind. Was a quieter dog a gentler dog? Could be. It seemed like a good start. And Tippy enjoyed tasty rewards for just watching the cats and not harassing them.

The cats seemed to gain confidence when Tippy was tied and quiet and didn't have freedom to patrol the house. The cats grew bolder, peering around couches and observing Tippy from the top of the fridge. We also gave the cats their own room, protected by a baby gate, allowing the cats an impenetrable refuge. Cats could go in and out under the gate. The Scottie couldn't.

The dog was slowly becoming more of a curiosity than a threat. BIG difference. You could almost hear Rigel saying to Sirrus and Vega, "So what are you guys doing tonight? Wanna go watch the dog? Let's get better seats than yesterday."

I had a few other ideas. I wanted the cats and dog to be comfortable with each other's scents, so I had Jim and Lois wipe their animals down and exchange the malodorous towels. Remember, animals are scent driven. In this case, familiarity bred content.

During the day, when Jim and Lois were at work, Jim brought Tippy to Lois's house and put him in his crate, allowing the cats to fully enjoy their space but further reinforcing that the dog was not a menace. When Jim and Lois were home together, the dog was always on the lead, usually tied to something, increasingly gaining more and more freedom, but dragging his cord and getting treats for his appropriate behavior.

Jim and Lois began to think that a blended family could be a reality. Perfect harmony was still a few months away, but progress was significant enough that they booked the caterer.

One day after the wedding, I got a call. It was Lois.

"Dr. Sampson, we all slept together last night. Even the three-legged cat jumped up on the bed. None of them were afraid."

For the first time in the age of Aquarius, all the stars were aligned.

DOG BITES

- Build your cat's confidence by reducing the opportunities your dog has to terrorize him.

- To control barking, use a stream of water in your dog's face following a QUIET command. It doesn't hurt, but it sure works.

- When introducing dogs and cats in the same household, the more they can see each other and positively interact, the better the chance for harmony.

—————— Chapter 26 ——————

HERD OF CATS

The call that day came from Mrs. Habersham. She was a busy woman, what with four kids, a dog, and three cats.

"I think we have a problem with Whiskers," she told me. "Whiskers is our two-year-old Border collie. It's kind of a peculiar problem."

"Oh, I've pretty much heard it all," I told her. "After fifteen years, you can't surprise me. What is your dog doing?"

"He's herding the cats."

Okay, I hadn't heard it all. I sure had never heard of a cat-herding dog. But it was true. Whiskers was in many ways a traditional Border collie: steely-eyed, resolute, and, when given the opportunity, somewhat of a workaholic.

Have you ever heard of someone saying to a workaholic: "Stay home, relax, take a load off." It doesn't work for people—and it doesn't work for Border collies.

In effect, that's exactly what they were doing to Whiskers. When Mrs. Habersham went off to work or to school events, Whiskers stayed in his crate. He didn't want to be in the crate. Like any workaholic, he wanted to go to his office and catch up on some paper work. (This is probably a bad metaphor—Whiskers was completely housebroken.)

When the family returned home, Whiskers shot out of the crate like a cannonball. Like a man granted parole, he wasn't sure where to turn first when released from confinement. Yes, that's when he started herding the cats, an activity that had all the neighbors talking, not to mention the cats. He would also herd the neighbors' kids when they were at the house, coercing them into one area of the backyard and circling them like they were so many sheep.

Whiskers became meticulous with his toys, constantly separating his stuff from the kids' stuff. He put everything back where it belonged in little piles. He was a real neatnick. Sadly, none of the kids, nor Mrs. Habersham's husband, exhibited these same traits.

The dog also became obsessed with his tennis ball when he was out of the crate. He'd take it to the top of the stairs, release it, and then chase it to the bottom. He did this once (that's cute), then twice (how funny!), then the fiftieth time. Enough, already.

When the ball was finally put away in the drawer, Whiskers stared at the bureau. He wanted that ball in the worst way.

While I had never seen a dog herd cats, Whiskers's high energy, especially for a Border collie, was certainly not unusual. Whiskers was basically stimulus-deprived. His long evolutionary history as a workhorse (workdog, we should say) meant that he required constant activity.

While I am a huge advocate of the crate in training dogs, I cautioned the owners about putting Whiskers back into the crate when his over-activity got on their nerves. Dogs are not stupid (neither are cats—I don't want to play favorites here) and you don't want your dog to think of the crate as punishment. The whole beauty of crate training is that your dog sees the crate as a home, a place he wants to sleep and rest in, not as a place he is put for being a BAD DOG!

The solution to this problem was pretty much common sense (I still charge the same amount). Whiskers needed far more exercise, more mental stimulation, some extra-curricular activity, and more new toys to keep life interesting. I suggested a Frisbee, a good choice because it gave Whiskers a chance to run, jump, chew, chase, and cavort. He just loved it.

I also suggested that Whiskers go back to obedience school and agility training, not because he was misbehaving, but because it was a good opportunity to further channel his work ethic into something challenging and constructive. Herding cats is fun, but it has no real lasting benefit to society.

Whiskers started to mellow a bit. A little more freedom, additional time outside the crate, and a somewhat scheduled exercise program allowed Whiskers to cool his jets. I haven't heard from Whiskers's owners in quite awhile. Rumor has it that Whiskers still had a great deal of excess energy, so he opened a small freelance business chasing geese off golf courses.

DOG BITES

- Redirect a dog's focus in a positive way with toys or treats to prevent unacceptable behavior.

- Dogs need lots of physical and mental stimulation.

—————— **Chapter 27** ——————

THE TWO FACES OF MIKE

I hope this story is helpful to people who have wondered why their dog sometimes acts like two different dogs. In my practice over the years, I have spoken to more than a few people who have claimed their dog has a multiple personality. At times, the dog may be shy and reclusive; other times the pooch is confident, even aggressive. How can that be? Why would that be?

Let's talk about an actual case. Mike was a Brittany spaniel. Having a human name* was not the only goofy thing about this dog. Mike was born with an abundance of energy, so much so that when his owners returned from work, he would burst out of his crate with such intensity it actually frightened Rex and Sheila. (It was Rex who named the dog Mike. Are things beginning to make sense?)

This alone was not that unusual. If you were in a crate all day, you'd have pent-up energy, too. But this was extreme. The initial concern was that the dog would lose respect for his home. Instead of seeing it as a quiet place, he began to associate his release and his hyperactivity with the inside of the house and with Rex and Sheila, his pack members. Not an association you want.

In addition, the dog was so energized and attention-seeking that he also began inappropriate "mouthing," grabbing his owner's arm or hand in his lightly clenched teeth. Mike was not biting, but this activity should not be encouraged by dog owners, lest the dog become confused where the line between play and aggression really is.

Rex and Sheila would eventually let Mike outside, where his dynamite personality could really ignite. Mike would make a beeline for the fence, where he tore up and down the boundaries of the yard for a long time. His tirade each day varied by so little that he created a trench along the fence line from his constant running back and forth. When it rained, Rex and Sheila had a moat around their house.

But despite all this energy, Mike was really asocial—fearful and shy around strangers. This was especially evident when the dog was alone in the yard. But if Rex or Sheila were with him, Mike suddenly became more confident, assertive, even aggressive. He had the backup of his pack members.

Very strange, huh? Not really.

In most cases, the explanation is simple. Dogs are pack animals, like the wolves they descended from. Animals in packs evolved to respect (but sometimes compete for) a position in the social order. Mike became emboldened by other members of his pack. The reticence that he felt when alone changed to conviction when accompanied by a fellow pack member. In this case it really was a fellow. It was Rex. Or a fellowess—Sheila.

There were multiple issues here, but first and foremost I wanted Rex and his wife to reclaim their home as a calm place. I suggested a vigorous outside exercise program of walks and ball playing each evening so that when Mike was brought back into the house, his first order of business was a nap. Great news because a tired dog is a good dog. Again, as in so many cases, the key is for the dog to make an association between a place and an activity.

Yard: Run, play ball, knock yourself out.

House: Eat, sleep, relax.

When Mike came back inside, he was also put on a lead and attached to a "tie-down," like a doorknob or table leg, and given treats. I wanted Mike close to his owners so that Mike would not think his return to the house was in some way a punishment. Mike needed to learn to stifle any energy that remained and cool his jets. And with no opportunity to race around the house, the nap seemed a good alternative.

After a couple of weeks, Mike was downgraded from hurricane to tropical storm, but the conditioning was taking awhile. To tweak things a bit, I suggested a water squirt bottle and a well-placed stream in the face when Mike got mouthy. This in an incredibly effective tool because most dogs just hate a squirt of water in the schnoz; however, it's more painful to the pride than the proboscis.

To further socialize Mike to people, he was walked and given treats by neighbors, and we encouraged everyone from the FedEx man to the mailman to do likewise. The treats re-directed his attention away from his fear to interest in people and "what's in it for me."

The UPS woman even started bringing her own homemade treats. It didn't take long for Mike to realize what brown could do for him.

* *I do not recommend giving dogs human names. The dog doesn't mind, but one day someone in a coffee shop will overhear you say: "We keep Tommy in a cage at night, and he hardly ever cries." When the police ring your doorbell, make sure Tommy has his collar on.*

DOG BITES

• Your dog should not think a tie-down is punishment. It's a time for him to relax, chew a favorite toy, and unwind. It's like your boss having you take a vacation in Bermuda.

• Dogs see the entire world through this lens: "What's in it for me." Some people also behave that way, but for dogs it's 100 percent.

————— **Chapter 28** —————

LICKITY SPLIT

"Dr. Sampson, my dog is constantly passing gas, and I don't know which way to turn."

Was that a serious complaint, I wondered, or just a great straight line? It was no joke. Their veterinarian had made several diet changes for the dog to no avail, so he had referred the family to me for behavior management.

Elliot was a big, burly sheepdog with paws like baked hams, who loved to lounge around the house and pass gas. It was not the kind of problem I usually get involved with, but the Eggelston family had a second issue with Elliot. He was constantly licking—licking everything. He licked the carpet, he licked himself, he licked Arnie and Betsy, the other two sheepdogs in the Eggelston family. Yes, these were all problems, especially since the Eggelstons and the three dogs all slept on the same king-sized bed.

Usually a behavior like constant licking is the result of boredom and the need for redirection and exercise. Dogs that become compulsive about one particular activity are frequently seeking attention or trying to relieve stress in another area of their lives.

For Elliot, the stress was probably related in part to

Arnie. The three-year-old sheepdog was clearly the alpha dog, but it wasn't quite as clear to Elliot as it should have been. Elliot was the runner-up and found that position a bit distasteful. He aspired to a higher place in life. As mentioned, Elliot was also a real attention-seeker, and the licking was his easiest tactic. If something would stay still long enough, Elliot was prepared to give it a good shellacking with his tongue.

Originally, Elliot had been directing his compulsion toward the carpet, but when the Eggelstons confined Elliot to an area in the house with no carpet, he licked himself instead. Mr. or Mrs. Eggelston would then reach down and distract him by calling his name or stroking him. Here's another classic case where the response to a problem by the owner can actually make things worse. From Elliot's standpoint, he was being rewarded—talked to, touched, and stroked—when he licked himself. That reinforced the licking. That was the attention he was seeking. Still, punishing him for the compulsion would have been even worse—adding stress to a problem that already had stress as a root cause.

And proof that the compulsion was attention-driven was that when the Eggelstons confined Elliot to a non-carpeted area while they were gone, they'd return to discover that he had not been licking himself. He was, excuse the canine expression, dry as a bone.

Now what about that gas problem? As I said, I try to keep my nose out of those more medically-based issues. Following much discussion, the Eggelstons and I made an interesting discovery: The gas problem was related to his licking, a not-so-surprising conclusion, since he was taking in a lot of air with each tongue swipe, especially when he licked himself. The Eggelstons also noticed that Elliot licked himself only if he was lying on his chest, like a library lion.

Knowing this, we taught Elliot to lie on his side on command when he was resting near the Eggelstons, thus breaking the compulsive cycle. We added lots of exercise, chew toys stuffed with treats, and other distractions. When the Eggeltons did catch him licking, they instructed him to lay on his side.

Ultimately, the compulsive behavior ceased. When I spoke to the Eggelstons months later, I learned that they had purchased a queen-sized bed, which they had nestled next to their king-sized bed so the entire family could sleep together more comfortably.

Unfortunately, Elliot could not shake his previous gastro-intestinal reputation and ended up with the queen bed all to himself.

DOG BITES
- Be sure that when you touch or pet your dog, you are reinforcing appropriate behavior.

- Refocus your dog's attention when he is involved in undesirable behavior.

—————— **Chapter 29** ——————

SAM THE SHAM

I bet you are wondering how my own pets behave. I bet you are thinking that because I have twenty years' experience counseling people about their dogs and cats, that my animals are perfectly disciplined, models of poise in the feline and canine community.

Oh, you weren't thinking that? Well, someone has a big mouth, then.

Our first three years with Sam the cat were pretty uneventful—no problems that would have prompted me to call someone like *me* on the phone.

True, Sam was needy: laps and loving 8/7 (That's like 24/7, but cats sleep at least 16 hours a day). Sam demanded constant attention with a crabby cry. When my wife, Elaine, was doing the crossword puzzle, there was Sam on her lap, four feet across, one head down. Elaine, like many pet owners, responded to the cat's wiles and thus created a controlling feline who became cranky if he didn't get his way—and who knew how to get exactly what he wanted. He was a high-maintenance cat.

When Liesel, a schnauzer puppy, entered the family, it seemed like we might get a reprieve from the clinginess.

The cat and dog bonded immediately, and their antics together were a source of great amusement to Elaine and me. A favorite activity of Liesel as she grew was to grab Sam by the head and neck and drag him along the slippery kitchen floor. Sam loved it and spent most of his life full of Liesel's slobber. They were soul mates. As you'll see, maybe they should have been inmates.

As Liesel was being housebroken, she discovered that when she returned to the front door (with Sam right behind her), Elaine provided them both with a treat. The treat-giving was supposed to be a reward for Liesel's adherence to traditional housebreaking requirements, but as I have mentioned in this book several times, animals cannot make that association. To them, the reward is for coming to the front door—not for proper potty procedure.

I hate to admit this, but the dog and cat soon conditioned both of *us*. I knew we were being manipulated, my wife knew we were being manipulated, and the dynamic duo knew we were being manipulated. It reached a point where Sam would cry to go out the back door many times a day, then show up at the front door sixty seconds later. Liesel would be in tow, both running to the pantry door to beg for treats. Not that they deserved it. They hadn't done their business, unless their business was fooling Elaine and me.

In the spring, when daylight came earlier, it was not uncommon for Sam to cry at the door around 4:30 in the morning. My wife would get up and let the little schemer outside. He would come back a few minutes later and get a treat. Elaine would go back to bed. In twelve-step programs I think they call this enabling.

Finally, we agreed enough's enough. "The cat has a litter box. Let's have Sam use it." Because Elaine was already on the edge with this cat, she didn't want to interrupt the delicate balance between the cat's demands and her own sanity. She wanted to leave bad enough alone. The tension between my wife and the crabby, demanding cat gave Elaine TMJ, which I can't prove, but we know this: When the cat died, the disorder cleared up.

It was time to put my experience to good use. Finally.

So whenever the cranky cry from Sam was heard at the front door in the middle of the night, I went and quickly picked him up and deposited him in the garage. I'm not one who sees human qualities in dogs and cats, but you should have seen the expression on Sam's face. After a few mornings with that approach, Sam got the picture, and his early morning requests to exit the house stopped.

And to further strengthen this reconditioning, Elaine and I promised each other to accompany Liesel when she needed to go out during the day so that she could be rewarded at the appropriate time, not when she returned to the front door.

At some point in all of this, we changed Sam's name to Grabis, a more fitting label, we thought, for a crabby, cranky cat that had managed, at least for a while, to live in a house with a supposed expert in pet behavior and his wife, and still twist them around his little paw.

You have to admit, I was very honest to acknowledge this. I was also very smart to do it in the last chapter.

DOG BITES

- If you don't shape your dog's behavior, the dog will shape yours.

- Only reinforce behaviors that you can live with forever.

- A reward must follow immediately after the behavior you want to encourage. Quickly admonish behavior you want to discourage.

ABOUT THE AUTHORS

Gary R. Sampson, DVM, is a native of Minnesota and a 1960 graduate of the University of Minnesota Veterinary School. He opened a private veterinary clinic while also serving as the Director of Mayo Research Animal Care Facilities at the University of Minnesota's School of Medicine. He moved to Indianapolis in the '60s and spent thirty-one years in animal products research management at Eli Lilly and Co. He also has authored numerous scientific publications. Dr. Sampson has devoted the last twenty years to helping beleaguered pet owners with their problem dogs and cats, although his work is mostly correcting the owners' behaviors.

Dr. Sampson lives in Indianapolis with his wife, Elaine, and Lizzie, their standard poodle. He has two children and three grandchildren who, unlike some of his patients, are all perfectly behaved.

Dick Wolfsie has worked in television and radio for more than twenty-five years and is currently a features reporter for WISH-TV in Indianapolis. An Emmy Award winner, he is the author of seven books, including *Barney: The Stray Beagle Who Became a TV Star and Stole Our Hearts*. Dick's weekly humor column is syndicated in twenty-five newspapers in central Indiana. He lives in Indianapolis with his wife, Mary Ellen, his son, Brett, Toby the beagle, and Benson the cat.

Books of Interest

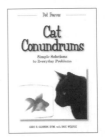

Also in the Pet Peeves series:
Cat Conundrums: Simple Solutions to Everyday Problems

Meet Ching, who inventively protested the family poodle's use of his litter box. Or Honey, who, in the absence of hockey pucks, expressed her athletic prowess in a most unsavory way. Cat owners will applaud Dr. Gary Sampson's creative approach to solving even the most purr-plexing feline behavioral issues.

In the *Pet Peeves* series, veterinarian Gary Sampson uses real-life examples from his experience as an expert in pet behavior to help you correct your pet's bad habits. These stories will have you laughing along and, more important, will leave you a bit wiser when it comes to establishing appropriate behavior in your furry friend.

Paperback   Price $9.99
ISBN: 1-57860-227-0

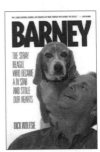

Barney
The Stray Beagle Who Became a TV Star and Stole Our Hearts
By Dick Wolfsie

The greatest Barney moments, told by his faithful human sidekick—a book destined to make dog lovers laugh, cry, and howl at the moon.

When TV Reporter Dick Wolfsie took in the tiny stray beagle shivering on his front step, he had no idea that the dog would become more than just a faithful companion. Barney the Beagle's career in the public eye included three thousand shows, fourteen commercials, and twelve straight years on the air.

If you followed Barney's antics over the years, you'll recognize your favorite Barney stories here, plus more than a few surprises. If you missed Barney on TV, here's your chance to meet an unforgettable beagle who had heart, brains, and moxie to spare.

Paperback   Price $14.99
ISBN: 1-57860-167-3